Bullying

Bullying

From Backyard to Boardroom

editors

Paul McCarthy
Jane Rylance
Robin Bennett
Helga Zimmerman

The Federation Press
2001

Published in Sydney by

The Federation Press
71 John St, Leichhardt, NSW, 2040
PO Box 45, Annandale, NSW, 2038
Ph: (02) 9552 2200 Fax: (02) 9552 1681
E-mail: info@federationpress.com.au
Website: http://www.federationpress.com.au

National Library of Australia Cataloguing-in-Publication data:

Bullying: from backyard to boardroom

Includes index
ISBN 1 86287 392 5

1. Bullying – Australia. 2. Aggressiveness (Psychology) – Australia. I. McCarthy, Paul.

302.540994

Typeset by The Federation Press, Leichhardt, NSW.
Printed by Southwood Press Pty Ltd, Marrickville, NSW.

Preface

This completely new edition of *Bullying: From Backyard to Boardroom* presents a collection of recent research findings and practice mainly in the Australian context, but also includes European benchmarks. The papers assembled by the editors cater for an evolution in readers' understandings since the release of the first edition in 1996. This initial publication, and others associated with the Beyond Bullying Association (BBA), have played a significant role in the growth of awareness about bullying in the adult sphere and the development of guidelines in Australia.

In the years since its publication, a more sophisticated awareness of the complexity and heterogeneity of bullying experiences has emerged, particularly in relation to the phenomenon as it occurs within the workplace. In these circumstances, readers now reasonably expect more research-based, substantiated information. In meeting that demand, the new edition moves beyond basic definitions, awareness, stories and remedies, that were common in earlier publications.

This edition may advantage people who have experienced the phenomenon, management and various organisational staff support bodies, educators, State legislative bodies and unions. For those experiencing bullying, understandings of its nature and practical remedies may be found in several chapters. Insights into bullying, across age, gender, employment and sector, are also useful for those motivated to assist others experiencing bullying. Indeed, research in progress by the editors indicates that targets of bullying frequently seek out such assistance.

The growth of awareness of bullying and its individual and organisational consequences has also presented management with the responsibility of dealing with the corrosive effects of bullying on employees' productivity and wellbeing. This new edition assists managers in addressing their concerns as to whether anti-bullying measures are necessary, proven to work, and cost-effective. The evidence presented in the book also updates the knowledge and skills of a range of organisational officers now more likely to be involved in procedures to address bullying. In these terms, the book is an important resource for human resource managers, equity and sexual harassment officers, counsellors, employee assistance providers, health and safety officers, union representatives, mediators, chaplains and trainers.

Whilst the first edition of *Bullying: from Backyard to Boardroom* proved a useful reference in educational curricula in Australia, England, Ireland the USA and Thailand (in translation), the new edition now provides an updated base for educators. Bullying is now an emergent theme for educators in a variety of disciplinary areas, including management, training and development, education, occupational health and safety, employee relations, corporate social responsibility, organisational psychology, interpersonal skills, social work, counselling, health and behavioural sciences, nursing, justice studies and the law. Educators in these areas now more commonly include reference to bullying in their curricula.

Authorities now more commonly express concerns about bullying in relation to their key legislated interests, that is, about bullying that occurs in conjunction with racism, discrimination, sexual harassment, hazardous work practices, unfair dismissal, rorting and corruption. This new edition provides a useful source of information for staff development with respect to bullying and its links with workers' compensation, discrimination, health and safety, human rights, health rights, workplace relations, electoral matters and criminal justice.

Several unions, most recently the Australian Council of Trade Unions (ACTU), have recognised bullying as a pressing concern in contemporary workplaces. A growing number of organisations now have bullying clauses within their codes of conduct. Union representatives are now routinely involved in offering advice to members about the issue, pursuing grievance procedures, taking cases to the industrial commission, assisting with legal action, and providing personal support. In addition, union officials and employee representatives are now commonly involved in negotiating inclusion of anti-bullying provisions in enterprise bargaining agreements.

The first edition, and other publications by the BBA, have been of widespread use in the formation of understandings, policies and practices in many of the areas of concern outlined above, as citations indicate. However, research and practice have since moved on, and the new edition updates these concerns. The editors recommend the book as an important reference for individuals, organisations, and authorities seeking substantiated information about the nature of bullying and preventive measures.

The Editors

Contents

Contributors

Cara Beed is a Melbourne academic sociologist with a particular interest in questions of power and abuse in religious organisations.

Vaughan Bowie is an author, consultant and academic at the University of Western Sydney. He has written a book (*Coping with Violence: A Guide for the Human Services*, Sydney: Karibuni, 1989) and a trainer's manual (*Coping with Violence: A Trainer's Manual*, Sydney: Karibuni, 1993), and has contributed articles to a number of journals on the topic of workplace violence.

Trish Bulbeck is a social worker who has worked with older people for many years. Her work has mainly been in the area of aged health, and she enjoys the challenge of establishing new services such as the Elder Abuse Prevention Unit in Queensland. Since 1997, Trish has been the Oceania Representative on the International Network for the Prevention of Elder Abuse. She recently became a Fellow of the Australian Association of Gerontology.

Peter Gorman is a barrister with a special interest in bullying at work, and the author of several monographs and book chapters addressing the legal aspect of this problem.

Michael Kennedy is a former detective now completing postgraduate studies at the University of Western Sydney, and was a consultant to the ABC, on the *Wildside* series among others.

Paul McCarthy has produced a number of publications addressing bullying at work, as author, co-author and co-editor. He is a lecturer in the School of Management at Griffith University.

Greg McMahon is a management consultant and trainer.

Cath Rafferty is the Manager of the Queensland Working Women's Service. She has been a leader in raising the issue of workplace bullying, and in the development of anti-bullying policies for industry and the provision of employee assistance to victims in Australia.

Ken Rigby is an associate professor at the University of South Australia. He is also an internationally acclaimed researcher who has conducted several major studies of school bullying.

Jane Rylance is a social worker engaged in employee assistance work. This research forms part of her PhD studies in the School of Social Work and Social Policy, at the University of Queensland.

Michael Sheehan is an author, editor and researcher of several books, research reports and journal articles, and he has established an international reputation as a researcher in the area of workplace bullying. He is a senior lecturer in the School of Management at Griffith University.

Fiona Underwood has been working at the University of South Australia since 1996. In this time she has co-ordinated subjects in human resources management and taught a range of sociology, politics, education and philosophy subjects. She has co-authored numerous published works, mostly in the area of workplace learning, and is currently completing a master's degree in education by research on the topic of learning from workplace violence. This is her first sole authored published chapter.

Dieter Zapf is internationally renowned for his research in the areas of stress and mobbing (bullying) at work. He is a professor in the Department of Psychology at the University of Frankfurt, Germany.

The Bullying Challenge

Paul McCarthy and Jane Rylance

The significance of this new edition is perhaps best demonstrated through locating it within the interplay of knowledge and interests that continues to drive the evolution of understandings of bullying in Australia. This is perhaps best achieved by initially providing a contextual overview of the international research that has assisted greatly in ensuring the entry and positioning of bullying as an ongoing concern in the public arena. Bullying as a phenomenon has been most developed in the school context, where it has been constructed as a recognised problem among school children and young people in Australia and internationally. Knowledge from this context has provided the springboard for research and understandings in the adult organisational sphere in the past decade. Indeed, the first chapter in this book by Ken Rigby on school bullying launches the following chapters, which then turn their attention to bullying in the adult arena, particularly within the workplace.

In the adult context however, research, understandings and interventions are still somewhat embryonic (Einarsen, 2000a; 2000b; Hoel et al, 1999). Thinking about understandings of bullying as formations, or configurations, that shape and are shaped by an interplay of diverse knowledges and interests, assists appreciation of the ways research and thinking have evolved in the area. Thus, the first decade of research on the phenomenon witnessed a proliferation of studies on definitional issues, incidence, causal factors, consequences and descriptive dimensions of the experience, and these mainly focused on the individual who had experienced the bullying (see Einarsen, 2000a; Hoel et al, 1999, for a review of these). This decade could arguably be characterised as a configuration of thought that recognised bullying as a single 'objective' entity with mono-causal factors and mono-dimensional characteristics (see Rylance, Chapter 3, this volume). Australia did not feature significantly in this first wave when compared with the countries that were well represented (for example, Sweden, Scandinavia and more recently, the UK). Only a handful of small, non-representative studies examining incidence and dimensions have occurred in Australia.

This first formation of research and thinking has also been characterised by a 'crisis-like' response to the growing awareness emanating from anecdotal and empirical research as to the detrimental individual and (speculated) organisational costs of bullying (for a summary of these consequences, see Einarsen, 2000a; 2000b; and Hoel et al, 1999). Thus, in numerous countries, including Australia, guidelines, policies, legislation and therapeutic interventions have been implemented to differing degrees at the individual, organisational and state level. These activities, however, have not been underpinned by comprehensive and directly relevant empirical research. Nor have they been evaluated. Rather, other theoretical frameworks from management, stress, organisational behaviour (Hoel et al, 1999), school bullying and other abuses have been utilised in their development. This perhaps has provided the foundation for Einarsen's (2000a) recommendation that the essential objectives of research in this area should be to assist in the preventive, management and healing dimensions.

Arguably, this call for research in the area, as well as other discussions around the construction and meaning of bullying, its 'processual' and dynamic dimensions, signals a second configuration of understandings and research, which appears to be emerging internationally (see Rylance, Chapter 3, this volume). This formation is characterised by a shift towards complexity, multi-dimensionality, and an exploration of 'subjectivity', and the construction and meaning of the phenomenon (for example, see Archer, 1999; Crawford, 1999; Einarsen, 2000b; Hoel et al, 1999; Zapf, Chapter 2, this volume). Furthermore, it is characterised by a valuing of a diversity of perspectives and methodological approaches resulting from emerging interests across professional disciplines. This has resulted in a call for studies exploring the perspectives of others involved in the bullying dynamic other than the target.

Bullying: From Backyard to Boardroom aims to contribute to this second configuration of thinking and research, and highlights the diversity of emergent interests in bullying in Australia. What follows is a coverage of the current 'state of play' with research and interventions in Australia. Given the diversity in the network of interests, these exchanges are complex, less linear, and more mutually reflexive, and the debate moves on several fronts at once. The sketch of these relationships that follows provides a basis for demonstrating the value of contributions to the new edition.

Emergent Interest in Bullying in Australia

The first conference to address the full spectrum of concerns about bullying, across schools, workplaces and institutions in Australia, was held by the Beyond Bullying Association in 1994. At this stage studies on school bullying were a fairly well-developed phenomenon, whilst the study of bullying in the adult arena (particularly in Australia) was in its infancy. Incidence studies were already occurring in Sweden (see Leymann, 1996, for a summary of his earlier findings). This forum began a process of mutual recognition of the strong similarities of bullying in our schools, workplaces and institutions. These concerns were infused with those of international keynote speakers and literature from the UK and Scandinavia, with local research into school bullying, and with experiences of many in workplaces undergoing restructuring.

The rise of the notion of workplace bullying as a new construction of difficulties at work highlighted a form of violence that generally fell outside legislative provisions for assault, sexual harassment and discrimination, yet was recognisable in terms of generally accepted connotations of bullying and abuse. Diffusion of the notion of workplace bullying has thus been enabled by understandings of school bullying, and other forms of abuse, for example, of psychological abuse in domestic violence and sexual harassment. The sharing of these concerns also contributed to the climate in which the first survey questionnaire of workplace bullying in Australia proceeded, with funding from WorkSafe Australia (McCarthy et al, 1995). Thompson's (1997) study for the South Australian Women's Centre extended this initial research.

Since then, the number of studies completed in Australia has been small, but continues to grow, using a diversity of methodologies from a diversity of perspectives. Australia, in particular, has conducted a number studies focusing on specific industries. For example, studies of bullying have been completed in nursing (Hockley, 1998), social service work (see Rylance, Chapter 3, this volume), construction (Barker et al, 1999), pastoral care (Beed and Beed, 1998), bullying by email in universities (Joseph, 1998), Olympic support services (Bowie, 2000), bullying of flight attendants (Williams, 2000), and in the masculine space of the courts (Hunter, 2000). In 1998, Janice Mayes and Chris Whiting published results of a study of bullying experienced at work by callers to an Australian Services Union (ASU) hotline who were predominantly female. The Australian Council of Trade Unions' (ACTU) survey of members' experiences of bullying at work was released in November 2000. At the time of writing, the most recently published study of bullying in Australia has been Oonagh Barron's (2000a) analysis of responses by callers to Job Watch.

The Diversity of Interests Driving the Debate

Throughout this time, the diversity of interests, their cross-fertilisation, and the leadership of women in driving the debate in Australia have been rkable. This interplay of interests has resulted in a variety of anti-bullying initiatives, including conferences and workshops, publication of guidelines, and taking of public stances at several nodes in the network. Now, the policies that address bullying in most Australian schools and school anti-bullying programs have provided templates for workplace policies. Working Women's Services in Queensland, South Australia and Tasmania have provided leadership in the development of guidelines, the conduct of research, the dissemination of information, and the provision of advice and counselling. The Premier's Council for Women in Queensland has been instrumental in funding development of a 'how to' manual for the implementation of anti-bullying guidelines by the Queensland Working Women's Service (QWWS, 2000). The Victorian Women's Trust also funded the Young Women and Workplace Violence Conference jointly organised by Job Watch and the Union Centre on Research and Technology in November, 2000.

Unions, of course, have also attempted to grapple with the complexities of how to respond to their members' concerns regarding bullying. The ASU, ACTU, National Tertiary Education Union, and the Australian Liquor, Hospitality and Miscellaneous Workers Union are among unions that have taken steps to address the problem of bullying. They have variously conducted research, opened help-lines, assisted with remedies, and promoted the inclusion of anti-bullying provisions in codes of conduct and enterprise bargaining agreements. The ACTU's (2000) health and safety campaign, 'The Workplace is No Place for Bullying', presents the most comprehensive union initiative so far in Australia. Their program is notable for its attention to types of bullying related to work organisation and management. These include unreasonable demands or impossible targets, restrictive and petty work rules, unfair rostering or allocation of work, being required to perform tasks without adequate training, and constant intrusive surveillance or monitoring. The ASU's concern with bullying, for example in relation to call centre management, has been eloquently expressed by Colin Lynch (2000).

These initiatives are positive, given research findings placing the extent of support sought from union representatives at a lesser status than from sources such as family, work colleagues and friends (McCarthy et al 1995; Thompson, 1997). The complexity, subjectivity and multi-dimensionality of the experiences of bullying challenge unions in responding to the phenomenon using their traditional processes. While bullying is a new concern for unions, the extent to which their assistance is perceived as helpful will no doubt be related to training of representatives, levels of support offered to members, the extent of inclusion of anti-bullying programs in enterprise bargaining agreements, and to proper monitoring and evaluation.

Legitimisation of concerns has also been forthcoming from anti-discrimination commissioners in Tasmania (Dr Jocelynne Scutt (2000)) and Queensland (Karen Walters) in their public stance against bullying. Shirley Stott-Despoya (2000) provides a compelling profile of ways that people experiencing deafness can be bullied in the most subtle ways, even in the guise of helping.

Associations representing concerned members of the public regarding issues directly and indirectly connected with bullying (such as the Beyond Bullying Association and the Whistleblowers) have actively promoted awareness of the problem. In addition, a number of professionals have also taken a public stance against bullying. They include doctors, psychiatrists, counsellors, psychologists, mediators, managers and members of the legal profession. To this can be added recent statements by General Cosgrove and the Australian Defence Forces generally, in their proclaiming 'zero-tolerance' of bullying in the defence forces.

Industry associations have also supported the implementation of anti-bullying policies. For example, *Risky Business* (QWWS, 2000), a manual for the implementation of anti-bullying policies, acknowledges the assistance of the Australian Industry Group, the Australian Mines and Metal Association, the Australian Sugar Milling Council, and the Furnishing Industry Association. Corporate interest is also evident through the contribution of Coles Supermarkets, Country Bake, Lockhardt Holden, Franklins, Meadow Lea Foods and others. These and other business interests that have fostered the implementation of preventive measures, are at the forefront of the growing realisation that bullying degrades productivity, health and wellbeing, and can allow corruption to persist.

The ferment of interest outlined above has variously manifested itself in, and been fuelled by, several sets of anti-bullying guidelines. The Queensland Division of Workplace Health and Safety's guide to workplace bullying (1998), in which Cath Rafferty of the Queensland Working Women's Service played a leading role, was the first of its kind in Australia. The QWWS's manual (2000), containing detailed advice for the implementation of these guidelines, has also been produced by Cath Rafferty. A practical handbook for the prevention of violence within organisations was written by Claire Mayhew (2000) for the Australian Institute of Criminology. The Office of the Employee Ombudsman of South Australia (2000) has released guidelines for the recognition and elimination of bullying in the workplace. The booklet 'Workplace Violence: Your Rights, What to Do and Where to Go for Help!' was written by Oonagh Barron (2000b) for Job Watch and the Victorian WorkCover Authority. The video and booklet, *No Bull: Say No to Bullying and Violence in the Workplace*, released by the Victorian Employers' Chamber of Commerce and Industry, and Job Watch (1999), is another ground-breaking initiative.

The judiciary and tribunals now routinely accept evidence of less overt, more subtle types of bullying in actions for unfair dismissal, psychological injury, negligence, and breaches of implied terms in employment contracts. While judgments in favour of plaintiffs in excess of $500,000 have been recorded, at least two have been overturned on appeals to higher courts. Given that the cycle of claim and counter claim in such cases can run for several years, the potential for this to compound the suffering for individuals who have already experienced trauma is evident. Thus far, a judgment of some $750,000 in favour of the plaintiff Seedsman against the New South Wales Police Service still stands. Gorman (1999) has noted that an antagonistic managerial climate was one factor mentioned in the judgment.

Initiatives to apply existing elements of the law more directly to bullying are also in evidence, for example, s 17(1) of the Tasmanian *Anti-Discrimination Act* 1998 makes specific reference to bullying behaviour that 'offends, humiliates, intimidates, insults or ridicules'. The Victorian WorkCover authority has also sued employees responsible for bullying a fellow worker for the recovery of the workers' compensation and reimbursement of medical costs awarded to the victim. Furthermore, the authority has fined a corporation $45,000 for 'failing to provide adequate information, instruction, training and supervision relating to the harassment and abuse of employees' (Cameron, 2000). An emergent trend to include anti-bullying provisions in enterprise bargaining agreements is also apparent. For example, the agreement between the University of Queensland Union (as employer) and the Liquor, Hospitality and Miscellaneous Workers' Union (2000) stand as a best-practice model for the incorporation of anti-bullying measures in an enterprise bargaining agreement.

The recent introduction of a Bill proposing an amendment to Queensland's *Public Service Act* 1996, which would constrain workplace harassment, including bullying, represents regulative advance. However, the regulation of bullying, in its complexity, remains difficult due to the lack of acceptable legal definition, as Dr Peter Patmore (2000), the Attorney General of Tasmania, has observed. Dr Patmore cautioned against the use of the law as a cure-all for social ills, warning of possible threats to its integrity through involvement in judgments about matters that escape legal definition. However, neither did he dismiss the possibility that legal definitions of types of bullying presently escaping legal constraint could be developed in future. Clearly, development of accessible legal remedies and their judicial interpretation may require the same timeframe as earlier regulation of forms of culturally and institutionally embedded violence such as domestic violence, sexual harassment, discrimination and stalking.

Notwithstanding the extent of guidelines available, the great majority of Australian organisations have yet to put in place policies that specifically mention bullying, particularly ones that would constrain more subtle, procedural forms of bullying. From the point of view of owners, boards of directors and managers preoccupied with market survival, this attitude is understandable. For most, bullying presently remains an optional concern within the domain of self-regulation. Mostly, bullying is not directly accounted for in corporate human resource information systems. Furthermore, given that Australia is behind other countries in its research of the phenomenon, statistically valid, random sample-based studies of incidences and costs of bullying in Australian workplaces, which would also inform management, have yet to be completed. Thus there is a lack of information to drive management to implement preventive measures.

Management concerns are also limited by the 'taboo' around speaking of bullying in organisations, as Einarsen (2000a) has noted. Indeed, the taboo may be linked with managerial prerogative, and with workplace cultures that allow bullying and abuse to persist. Also, the significant 'people skills' shortfall among Australian managers, identified by Karpin (1995), may well reduce sensitivities in management to bullying. Furthermore, in the dominant maleness of managerial realms, to identify oneself as a victim, even speak of concerns about bullying of others, may be self-stigmatising as a sign of weakness in the present corporate climate. As such, speaking of bullying may not sit well with job futures, since a certain male toughness may be prized up the line. In addition, there is also the fear that to speak of bullying could open an embarrassing can of worms. In many workplaces and institutions, where 'that is the way things are done around here', these predispositions tend to silence those who might feel concerned about bullying.

In Australia, as in other countries, policy development and the publication of guidelines have raced ahead of both research validation and the implementation and evaluation of preventive measures. In Australia, one reason for this is the anecdotal evidence that has emerged through the expression of public concerns about bullying, informally in stories, and in the media. This appears to have created a climate in which governments have seen the value in releasing guidelines as emblems of 'caring'. Notably, this 'crisis-like' response to bullying has been less dependent on empirical research findings, and more on the rising tide of community concerns and their networking to constrain unacceptable behaviours.

Perhaps indicative of this lack of research is the limited effectiveness of the proclaimed guidelines by several government agencies. Access to remedies by targets of bullying remains fraught with difficulty (McCarthy and Barker, 2000). Furthermore, a study by Barker and Sheehan (2000) has found evidence of difficulties that clients have experienced with their lawyers in the course of seeking legal remedies for bullying. More than half the interviewees reported lack of acknowledgment of the client or the situation, lack of experience or education about workplace bullying, and lack of professionalism among their legal representatives. These findings highlight the need for legal professionals to give consideration to special support, information, and communication needs of individuals experiencing bullying-related trauma.

The present difficulty in accessing remedies and the lack of progress in the implementation of preventive measures and their evaluation may well leave the medical-workers' compensation–legal route as the most commonly used one for seeking remedy for the distress of workplace bullying. In his chapter in this book, Zapf notes how some individuals adopt an 'over-achieving' role in an relentless fight for their rights. Furthermore, currently doctors write some nine million prescriptions for anti-depressants per annum. A recent study reported that the daily use of anti-depressants in Australia almost tripled in the 1990s and that Sweden was the only country to record a bigger increase. Most prescriptions were written by general practitioners, and the average daily dose per 1000 of population had increased form 12.4 in 1990 to 35.7 in 1998. An expert has attributed some half of these prescriptions to workplace conflict (Australian Broadcasting Commission, 2000; Parnell, 2000).

Thus, at present a significant risk is that the predominant source of treatment for the experience of bullying may well be located in the medicalisation of violence, of which Dr Jocelynne Scutt (1994) has written. Complex considerations are relevant here as to the responsibility of medical practitioners in these instances. The sharing of responsibility and action by the medical profession, workers' compensation and health and safety authorities, and targets of bullying may be required to break this emerging pattern. Doctors could well diagnose distress in ways that recognise contextual organisational contributions. They could also take steps to report these conditions to health and safety authorities in the interests of bringing statutory obligations into play, to address workplace hazards.

Unfortunately, with the tightening of definitions around 'psychological injury' in the workplace, workers' compensation authorities seem torn between recognising the implication of bullying in stress, psychological injury and pay-outs, and suppressing the abundant evidence they possess of this relationship. Certainly, airing the evidence these agencies have would provide a more substantiated basis for addressing the problem and the implementation of preventive measures. While this inaction continues, the problem will also continue to fester, and reduce the impetus of organisations to address the issue.

The release of statistical evidence of the implication of bullying in workers' compensation claims is also necessary to enable the costing of bullying's effects. These costs are likely to be substantial. Research in the UK points to the need for more systematic research into the costs of bullying, for example, a UK case study by Charlotte Rayner (2000) has modelled the potential costs of bullying in a 1000-strong workforce. Research benchmarks were applied that indicated between 10% and 20% of workers experience bullying and that one in four leaves as a consequence. Replacement of these employees was costed using industry averages at £15,000. On this basis, the replacement costs of bullying amount to £375,000. Rayner also estimated that if two other staff members were to observe each case of bullying and 20% of the observers leave, additional costs of £600,000 would be incurred. Furthermore, she cites evidence placing the cost of an internal investigation at £75,000, and that of defending action in a tribunal at £120,000.

Another indicator of the need to research the costs of bullying further may be found in a case study estimate that places the cost of bullying by a new manager in a 28-strong work team at $64,915 (QWWS, 2000). This estimate encompasses the costs of absenteeism, sick leave, lower morale and lower commitment in the work group, replacement of the staff member, retraining, and the costs of the loss of experience and investment in the staff member. Estimates of loss of sales due to a decline in public image, an investigation and an action for unfair dismissal are also included.

In the pattern of the evolution of understandings about bullying in Australia, research on school bullying by Associate Professor Ken Rigby of the University of South Australia reflects the more developed nature of understandings of and research on school bullying when compared to that of the workplace arena. Thus, he has validated concerns about school bullying and the effectiveness of preventive measures. However, research into workplace bullying remains at a formative stage, both in Australia and internationally. In these circumstances, publication of the small quantity of research completed in Australia, such as that in this edition, is important to extend understandings, substantiate claims, and justify investment in preventive measures. Studies in this edition of *Bullying: From Backyard to Boardroom* are significant in the way they variously contextualise, complement, extend and provide benchmarks for emergent research into bullying in Australia.

The Significance of the Authors' Contributions

In the first chapter, Associate Professor Ken Rigby draws on his leadership in researching school bullying in Australia. His work dispels myths that school bullying is predominantly physical and by males. Dr Rigby finds that verbal abuse, exclusion and social manipulation are the most frequent forms of abuse, thus aligning forms of school bullying with those identified in workplace studies. His charting of the cycle of deterioration in the interaction between the bully and the victim over time, to the point where the victim's failure to cope can incite further bullying, equates with Einarsen's (2000a) modelling of this process in workplaces. Thus, his research reflects the growing awareness of the 'processual' dimensions of the bullying experience both at school and in the workplace. Evidence that bullying contributes to psychological and physical ill-health at school is also compatible with research in the workplace.

At a time when the rate of suicide of young people surpasses the road toll, Rigby's identification of a higher rate of thoughts of suicide amongst victims of school bullying is a chilling reminder of the need for effective preventive measures. The author has a valuable message for the workplace: that progressive school bullying programs do work, that the method of 'shared concern' is a healthy developmental way of achieving behavioural change, and that effective programs are marked by the acceptance of responsibility by everyone in the school community.

Professor Dieter Zapf's chapter is of considerable interest, given the recognition of his scholarship in researching stress and mobbing (or bullying) at work. In light of European leadership in epidemiological studies of bullying, his review of European research provides important benchmarks for directions in Australia. Professor Zapf categorises bullying as an extreme social stressor that can have severe health consequences for victims. He confirms Leymann's definition, that for a behaviour to qualify as bullying (or mobbing) it should occur repeatedly (for example, once a week for at least six months). Commentaries on incidences of bullying, differences between bullying and mobbing, and the duration of bullying by the author are valuable. Another important element in his chapter is his comprehensive model of the complex multi-causal, multi-directional interplay of causes, behaviours and effects in workplace bullying. These understandings effectively move beyond simplistic explanations and signify a shift to the second wave of research and thinking about bullying. While Professor Zapf's model addresses the contentious issue of the interacting dynamic involved in bullying and of how the target's behaviour in some instances can influence bullying behaviours, he places the responsibility for the problem squarely with management.

The review of research in the first two chapters is followed by a number of industry and sector studies. Jane Rylance's study of bullying/abuse in the helping professions is the first of its kind in Australia. She has aimed to integrate both configurations of understandings in her research. Thus, she explores the subjective perceptions regarding what constitutes the phenomenon of 'bullying', whilst still adhering to some basic 'objective' criteria delineating the experience of others in the workplace in the reporting of her findings. Respondents to her survey suggest that experiences of bullying at work for a significant proportion pose significant contradictions to the ethos of caring in these professions. The study also provides new insights into the nature of bullying among women in a predominantly female profession. Her finding, that abuse at work by fellow employees and managers is an issue in addition to abuse by clients, also extends present perceptions of the problem. Furthermore, the implications of bullying in social service organisations in relation to the potential impact on clients are also briefly explored. The discussion of these findings is of considerable interest to managers and staff in a sector subject to ongoing pressures of welfare reform, marketisation and restructuring.

Michael Kennedy's study of the ways in which policing has led to the police being constructed as both bullies and victims in events surrounding recent commissions of inquiry in New South Wales is also unique. His mapping of systemic factors that construct the police as bullies breaks through the superficialities of the 'good cop/bad cop' binary purveyed by both the media and politicians, and uncritically accepted by the public. His approach reveals ways complex histories of economy, class and work role are embedded in the culture and organisation of policing.

In view of these complexities, Kennedy calls for more wisdom in the apportionment of blame, since mindless pursuit of the law, 'because the law is the law', can leave both the police and the public exposed to heavy-handed undemocratic behaviours. Appreciation of ways these factors can be implicated in the construction of the police as both bullies and victims is salutary for all of us concerned with bullying. It demonstrates how we can move beyond explanations commonly cast in terms of the familiar, the psychological and the individual, to deeper understandings of the complexities of bullying and more sustainable remedies.

Given widespread concerns about abuse in religious institutions, families and social networks, Cara Beed's chapter is timely. She speaks of cultures of abuse that continue to flourish in authoritarian organisations. In recognising difficulties in establishing accountability for abuse in these organisations, she calls for widespread public education on the nature of the problem, and a development of community sensitivity and the capacity to monitor the problem. Part of this awareness-building involves contrasting authoritarian relationships with authoritative relationships, which value personal autonomy and an open resolution of differences. The author's checklist of 35 factors for use in monitoring for cultures of secrecy and abuse in family, work, social services and community life, is highly useful as an audit device.

New ways of understanding bullying that extend present constructions of bullying are modelled in the next three chapters. Their focus on construction, meaning and subjectivity across the phenomenon provides an important parallel to the shift to the second configuration of research. In doing so, these chapters have important implications for theory and practice.

An innovative framework for the identification of bullying using organisational procedures is outlined in Greg McMahon's chapter. Procedural bullying is now being recognised as an increasingly prevalent form of bullying. The author's typology of types of procedural bullying and the manipulations of those who perpetrate them strips the veneer of legitimacy from organisational roles and procedures that often conceal their inherent bullying dynamic. His profile of the manipulation of compliance through reward and punishment, loyalty and disloyalty, and the implication of 'innocent parties', reveals procedural bullying for what it is – a shabby skills failure that is wildly incongruent with contemporary organisational missions and best-practice in management. Given the ways in which procedural bullying contributes to cultures of fear and compliance that decrease productivity and innovation, and can further corruption, the author's typology is pertinent. McMahon's proposals alert us to the formidable task ahead, that of 'recapturing organisational governance from bullies and their culture'.

Vaughan Bowie's profile of those who are directly involved in downsizing initiatives (the 'reluctant executioners'), indicates their experience of a range of ill-effects, including guilt, increased workload, organisational and social isolation, intense emotional, physical and behavioural pressure, and negative spill-over effects onto the family. The author writes of this misery, and its sharing among survivors, as a prologue for an examination of claims of downsizing. This chapter is important because it highlights the subjectivity of experiences and the differences across perspectives in dynamics perceived as bullying and indeed, alerts us to the complications in understanding and addressing the phenomenon. Furthermore, it reveals the perspective on the experience of those who are frequently labelled as the 'bully' in the context of organisations undergoing restructuring. This perspective turns on its head traditional ways of thinking about the person often cast in the role of 'bully' in these processes. Research is also cited that indicates downsizing is commonly faddish, ill-conceived, poorly planned and executed, and fails to achieve its aims.

Given the volume of research suggesting the misery of downsizing commonly leads to naught for all involved, constructive alternatives outlined in this chapter could well be prescribed reading for all those contemplating downsizing. The author's advice, for those of us who direct our anger at individual downsizers is worthwhile. That is, refocusing on systemic causes such as economic rationalism, and the advocacy of alternatives and the management training and development that goes with them, are likely to be more constructive in the longer term.

However, at the moment there is less research into ways experiences that give rise to emotional intensities might come to be seen as bullying and trigger action to work through the problem. These issue are becoming evident, however, in this second configuration of understandings and research of bullying. Fiona Underwood's chapter presents original qualitative research involving an innovative conceptual modelling, which adds a significant new dimension to our understanding of these issues. The moment of epiphany she identifies is one of a peak intensity of thought and emotion, or crisis, at which there is a transition to a new way seeing the familiar. Turning points she pursues in her research include the moment of realisation that one's experiences are of bullying, and the movement from self-perceptions saturated with fear to those based on empowerment in seeking redress. The author's application of this method in modelling ways a victim of bullying moves from negative to positive sensitivities at key defining moments creates a rich texture of explanation. Appreciation of the ways understanding of bullying moves at these turning points will no doubt assist with interventions at the levels of the individual and the organisation. This chapter highlights the importance of the 'processual' dimensions of bullying and offers insight into attributional processes in these experiences (see Hoel et al, 1999 for a discussion on attributional processes).

If bullying is a social construction, history teaches us to be vigilant about the limits of constructions of meaning around distressful experiences, meanings that can actually worsen the victimisation for those who adopt the meanings uncritically. Paul McCarthy's chapter maps the interplay of knowledge and interest in the cross-gender networking of resentment that has driven the rise of the discourse *bullying-at-work* and models it as a syndrome for the purpose of evaluating its limits. Key related concerns revealed in this process are the individualisation, psychologisation, medicalisation and legalisation of the experience of bullying in a professional–bully–victim triangle. The author's concern is that these establish the medical–workers' compensation–legal route as the main pathway for those seeking remedies.

Other issues discussed include: the problems in speaking of women as bullies in male-dominated spaces; the complex relations of victim-identity, complicity, masochism, self-sacrifice and human capacities for cruelty; and the limits of self-regulation guidelines as governmental emblems of caring, whilst Third-Way politics legitimates 'soft-violence'. Calls for the criminalisation of bullying are also seen to raise difficulties, due to the potential for Salem-like witch-hunts of the 'evil' in more subtle types of bullying that escape legal definition. The potential for the doubling of victimisation for those taking positions in the discourse at these points leads the author to call for the exercise of responsibility by professionals involved in constructing the syndrome.

The next four chapters are concerned with preventive strategies and the discussion includes innovative measures to address bullying at the levels of the individual, the organisation and the government. In the first of these two, Cath Rafferty outlines the ground-breaking efforts by the Queensland Working Women's Service (QWWS) to provide assistance to victims of workplace bullying. The QWWS's experience derives from their dealing with client complaints about workplace bullying, which have risen to some 1000 per year, representing 30% of their total complaints. The leadership of QWWS in networking community concerns into a program of awareness raising and action is to be applauded as a model of excellence. A tangible output of this action has been the development of the first State government guidelines in Australia to address bullying at work. The author outlines the content of these guidelines and the strategies they recommend for employers and employees, and at law. Given these guidelines currently serve as templates for preventive measures throughout Australia, and that they are now finding their way into enterprise bargaining agreements, codes of conduct and management strategies, they are of considerable interest.

Given that legal remedies are commonly proposed as the ultimate remedy for workplace bullying, or the necessary 'stick' to make other remedies work, Peter Gorman's review of systemic injustices that inhibit legal claims is important. Concerns raised by the author include: the difficulties faced by individuals suffering severe trauma in representing themselves in the pursuit of legal remedies; the lack of awareness and use of protocols in workplace agreements that would foster the early resolution of disputes; provisions in work cover Acts that inhibit early intervention and support and further the depression and anxiety common among victims of bullying; the failure of work cover authorities to stem the harmful consequences for applicants who incorrectly fill out complex forms; the lack of appropriate financial support during extended claim processes; and lengthy delays in the hearing of matters before tribunals. The professional, ethical and administrative failures implicated in these circumstances, as well as an estimate of extraordinarily high economic costs, justify the author's call for reform.

Dr Michael Sheehan takes an innovative approach by highlighting the responsibility of management in addressing bullying. He uses the frameworks of the twin benchmarks of professionalism and emotional intelligence to conceptualise these responsibilities further. His approach is systematic, in reviewing the role descriptors of management and the roots of managerial professionalism in the literature. Dr Sheehan demonstrates ways these descriptors provide the basis for the construction of managers as professionals by associations such as the Australian Institute of Management. Research findings indicating that employees experiencing bullying in organisations most commonly implicate managers as perpetrators are presented as evidence of departures from managerial professionalism.

In the light of the personal and organisational risks in this situation, the author calls for a program of action to reshape managers as professionals. The complementary development of people skills and emotional intelligence is proposed as a way to achieving this end. This also entails the development of skills such as active listening, expressive actions and interaction management, as well as abilities to recognise and differentiate one's own emotional state and that of others. Importantly, this approach adopts a responsible and respectful treatment of all concerned in the bullying process and does not call for punitive measures.

The final contribution, by Trish Bulbeck, addresses bullying and abuse in the context of the elderly, a problem that has aroused widespread community concern in recent years. Her chapter adds another important element to the mosaic of bullying in our institutions, workplaces and families, one that is of considerable concern given the increasing numbers in our population who are living longer. She outlines several factors in our culture, institutions and economy that cast the elderly as a high risk group in terms of exposure to bullying. These factors include physical and emotional dependency, ageism, workplace pressures, technological change and downsizing. The author reports research findings and case study material that demonstrate ways these factors contribute to neglect, mistreatment, exploitation and malicious acts that induce shame, loss of dignity and powerlessness. Her review of the status of preventive programs and legislation points to an urgent need to upgrade protection against the bullying and abuse of the elderly in Australia.

The Way Ahead

The outline of the concerns of contributors to this edition, as presented above, illustrates the direction in which the debate about bullying is being driven, on several fronts, and in a mutually furthering way. The diversity of theories, methodologies, industry and institutional studies, and remedies currently being brought to bear on the problem of bullying is remarkable. So, too, is the cross-section of interests, encompassing researchers, working women's services, employee assistance providers, lawyers, unions, managers, and educators represented among the contributors to *Bullying: From Backyard to Boardroom*. The ways in which this diversity enriches the debate and furthers the evolution of understandings and preventive measures are also apparent. This research has been able to use the initiatives in the school bullying arena as a springboard.

While this edition adds definition and relation to current understandings of bullying and preventive measures, the need for ongoing action to move beyond cul-de-sacs that inhibit access to effective remedies is also apparent. While valiant, largely under-resourced efforts are being made to address the problem in some quarters, the contributors highlight a number of other areas in which basic improvements to preventive and management strategies and access to remedies would be highly cost-effective. These need to occur at the individual, organisational and governmental levels.

The resourcing of programs to accelerate the implementation of health and safety guidelines at the organisational level, beyond their use as emblems of governmental or organisational caring, is one such initiative. Their independent evaluation is also important, if they are to be meaningful. Development of definitions and access to remedies for more subtle, procedural types of bullying, beyond those that are already illegal, such as assault, sexual harassment or discrimination, is also necessary.

Support for individuals seeking redress for the traumatic experience of bullying, from employee assistance agencies, within organisations, and from unions, requires further funding. Given that managers continue to loom large as those who are perceived to engage in bullying behaviours, the inclusion of studies of bullying in managerial skills development and related criteria in recruitment and appraisal are also worthwhile.

The integration of workers' compensation and health and safety concerns, basic reforms of claims procedures, and accountability for levels of workers' compensation premiums in relation to claims and to the effective operation of anti-bullying policies at divisional levels, all offer prospective cost-effective constraints on bullying. Given its costs, breaking the dominance of the medical-workers' compensation–legal pathway to redress has the potential to realise substantial economic and health benefits. Effective implementation of preventive measures within organisations and their independent evaluation would go some way to realising these benefits.

Further intellectual and emotional labour concerning the construction of bullying also appears worthwhile. In these terms, refocusing concerns, from psychologically inscribed victim identities, and narrow focus on individual perpetrators, to more systemic and cultural factors, may also lead to more comprehensive interventions. This is particularly so given the roots of bullying in economic rationalism and globalisation. Refocusing understandings along these lines can help further the healthy networking of resentments into collective action for change, locally and across a broad coalition of interests.

At the level of research into bullying at work, the need remains for funding and workplace access to enable completion of large scale random sample-based studies, using validated research instruments. Whilst such studies have been completed in Europe, they have yet to proceed in Australia. Research into costs of bullying and evaluation of the effectiveness of interventions, including guidelines, would help justify the wider implementation of preventive measures. Furthermore, research recognising and exploring the 'processual' elements and the dynamic interactions of bullying is also needed. This research should acknowledge the multiplicity of perspectives involved and be open to different theoretical and methodological approaches in their exploration. In addition, research on the perceptions and attributional processes inherent in bullying interactions is also important. Exploring these processes can assist in understanding the subjectivity and multi-dimensionality of the experiences of bullying. This perhaps underpins Einarsen's (2000b) assertion that incidence studies should explore these dimensions in addition to their usual foci.

The co-ordination of diverse interests around Australia also needs planning. The first canvassing of national guidelines to address bullying at work can be found in a seminal research report (McCarthy et al, 1995), funded by WorkSafe Australia. The proposal that there be a summit to develop national guidelines remains a possible option for a federal government willing to address the issue. A positive move towards the development of a national agenda for action has been a recent informal agreement between Job Watch, Queensland Working Women's Service and the Beyond Bullying Association to host a two-day workshop involving representatives of key State and federal interests in 2001.

References

ACTU (2000) 'The Workplace is No Place for Bullying', available at <http://www.actu.asn.au>.

Archer, D (1999) 'Exposing "Bullying" Culture in the Paramilitary Organisation' 20(1/2) *International Journal of Manpower* 94–105.

Australian Broadcasting Commission (2000) 'Background Briefing', Radio National, 23 May.

Barker, M and Sheehan, M (2000) 'Bully or Advocate: Reflections on the Lawyer–Client Relationship', in M Sheehan, S Ramsay and J Patrick (eds), *Transcending Boundaries: Integrating People, Processes and Systems*. Brisbane: School of Management, Griffith University.

Barker, M, Skas, E and Dyer, H (1999) 'Adult Workplace Bullying in an Australian Construction Organisation', in C Fraser, M Barker and A Martin (eds), *Organisations Looking Ahead: Challenges and Directions*. Brisbane: School of Organisational Behaviour and Human Resource Management, and School of Management, Griffith University.

Barron, O (2000a) *Working in Fear: Experiences of Workplace Violence*. Melbourne: Job Watch.

Barron, O (2000b) 'Workplace Violence: Your Rights, What to Do, and Where to Go for Help!' Melbourne: Job Watch and Victorian WorkCover Authority.

Beed, C and Beed, C (1998) 'Bullying in Pastoral Care', in P McCarthy, M Sheehan, W Wilkie and S Wilkie (eds), *Bullying: Causes, Costs and Cures*. Brisbane: Beyond Bullying Association.

Bowie, V (2000) 'Planes, Trains and Prostitutes: Dealing with Potential Violence Encountered by Olympic Support Services' 16(3) *Journal of Occupational Health and Safety Australia and New Zealand* 247–254.

Cameron, B (2000) 'New Strategies to Tackle Workplace Bullying', media release from the Minister for Local Government and Minister for WorkCover, Victoria, 18 October.

Crawford, N (1999) 'Conundrums and Confusion in Organisations: The Etymology of the Word "Bully"' 20(1/2) *International Journal of Manpower* 86–93.

Division of Workplace Health and Safety (Qld) (1998) *Workplace Bullying: An Employer's Guide*. Brisbane: Division of Workplace Health and Safety.

Einarsen, S (2000a) 'Bullying and Harassment at Work: Unveiling an Organisational Taboo', in M Sheehan, S Ramsay and J Patrick (eds), *Transcending Boundaries: Integrating People, Processes and Systems,* Brisbane: School of Management, Griffith University.

Einarsen, S (2000b) 'Bullying and Harassment at Work: A Review of the Scandinavian Approach' 5 *Aggression and Violent Behavior* 379–401.

Gorman, P (1999) 'Seedsman v State of New South Wales: Post-traumatic Stress Payout' 5 *Beyond Bullying News* 4–5.

Hockley, C (1998) 'The Cost of Silence: Women Bullying Women', in P McCarthy, M Sheehan, W Wilkie and S Wilkie (eds), *Bullying: Causes, Costs and Cures*. Brisbane: Beyond Bullying Association.

Hoel, H, Rayner, C and Cooper, C (1999) 'Workplace Bullying' 14 *International Review of Industrial and Organizational Psychology* 189–230.

Hunter, R (2000) 'Zealous Advocacy or Trial by Battle? Barristers as Courtroom Bullies'. Paper presented at It's Time to Make a Stand Conference, Anti-Discrimination Commission, 16–18 October, Hobart.

Joseph, R (1998) 'Electronic Mail and Petty Tyranny', in P McCarthy, M Sheehan, W Wilkie and S Wilkie (eds), *Bullying: Causes, Costs and Cures*. Brisbane: Beyond Bullying Association.

Karpin, D (1995) *Enterprising Nation*. Canberra: AGPS.

Leymann, H (1996) 'The Content and Development of Mobbing' 5(2) *European Journal of Work and Organizational Psychology* 257–6.

Lynch, C (2000) 'The Expression of Violence against Women'. Paper presented to the Young Women and Workplace Violence Conference, Job Watch and the Union Centre on Research and Technology, 27–8 November, Melbourne.

McCarthy, P and Barker, M (2000) 'Workplace Bullying Risk Audit' 16(5) *Journal of Occupational Health and Safety Australia and New Zealand* 409–18.

McCarthy, P, Sheehan, M and Kearns, D (1995) *Managerial Styles and Their Effects on Employees' Health and Well-Being in Organisations Undergoing Restructuring*. Brisbane: School of Organisational Behaviour and Human Resource Management, Griffith University.

Mayes, J and Whiting, C (1998) 'Bullying: Female Workers' Experience', in P McCarthy, M Sheehan, W Wilkie and S Wilkie (eds), *Bullying: Causes, Costs and Cures*. Brisbane: Beyond Bullying Association.

Mayhew, C (2000) *Preventing Violence within Organisations: A Practical Handbook* (Research and Public Policy Series No 29). Canberra: Australian Institute of Criminology.

Office of the Employee Ombudsman (2000) *Bullies Not Wanted: Recognising and Eliminating Bullying in the Workplace*. Adelaide: Office of the Employee Ombudsman of South Australia.

Parnell, S (2000) 'Antidepressant Use Soars in Australia', *Courier Mail,* 6 November, p 6.

Patmore, P (2000) Official Opening Address at the It's Time to Make a Stand Conference, Anti-Discrimination Commission, 16–18 October, Hobart.

Queensland Working Women's Service (QWWS) (2000) *Risky Business: A Useful Publication for Employers for Preventing and Resolving Workplace Bullying*. Brisbane: QWWS.

Rayner, C (2000) 'Building a Business Case for Tackling Bullying: Beyond a Basic Cost–Benefit Approach', in M Sheehan, S Ramsay and J Patrick (eds),

Transcending Boundaries: Integrating People, Processes and Systems. Brisbane: School of Management, Griffith University.

Scutt, J (1994) *The Sexual Gerrymander*. Melbourne: Spinifex.

Scutt, J (2000) 'Definitive Moments Capturing the Politics of Bullying' *Leading Issues Journal* (November). Available at <http://www.leadershipforwomen.com.au/leading%20issues/nov1.htm>.

Stott-Despoya, S (2000) 'Bullying and Deafness' *Leading Issues Journal* (November). Available at <http://www.leadershipforwomen.com.au/leading%20issues/nov1.htm>.

Thompson, C (1997) *Workplace Bullying Project*. Adelaide: Working Women's Centre of South Australia.

University of Queensland Union, and the Australian Liquor, Hospitality and Miscellaneous Workers' Union (2000) University of Queensland Union Certified Agreement. Queensland Industrial Relations Commission. No CA340 of 2000.

Victorian Employers' Chamber of Commerce and Industry, and Job Watch (1999) *No Bull: Say No to Bullying and Violence in the Workplace*. Melbourne: VECCI and JobWatch.

Williams, C (2000) 'A Pain in the Neck: Passenger Abuse, Flight Attendants and Emotional Labour' 16(5) *Journal of Occupational Health and Safety Australia and New Zealand* 429–36.

Chapter 1

Bullying in Schools and in the Workplace

Ken Rigby

The study of bullying and harassment has, in the past, focused mainly on relationships between children at school, largely, I think, because in that context bullying can be more readily observed and recorded. Hence our knowledge of bullying tends to be from studies of children at school. We need to ask ourselves whether such knowledge really helps us to understand what happens when adults bully other adults in the workplace or in the home.

We may feel that social situations at school and in the adult world are so different that what we have learned about interventions in relatively controlled, or controllable environments such as schools, may not apply when it comes to sorting out disputes between people at work. But is this so? In this chapter we will consider whether, in addressing bullying in the workplace, we can usefully draw on studies of bullying and harassment at school.

Definition

Bullying is repeated oppression, psychological or physical, by a more powerful person or group of persons (Rigby, 1996). It is not the same thing as aggression or violence, which can occur between people of equal strength or power. With bullying, one person or group is, by definition, more powerful than another. Most people see bullying as unjust or unfair.

Bullying at School

For many people the central feature of schoolyard bullying is male physical domination. This may seem a far cry from the kind of bullying that occurs in most workplaces or homes. But in fact, when we come to look

Figure 1.1 The bullying cycle begins

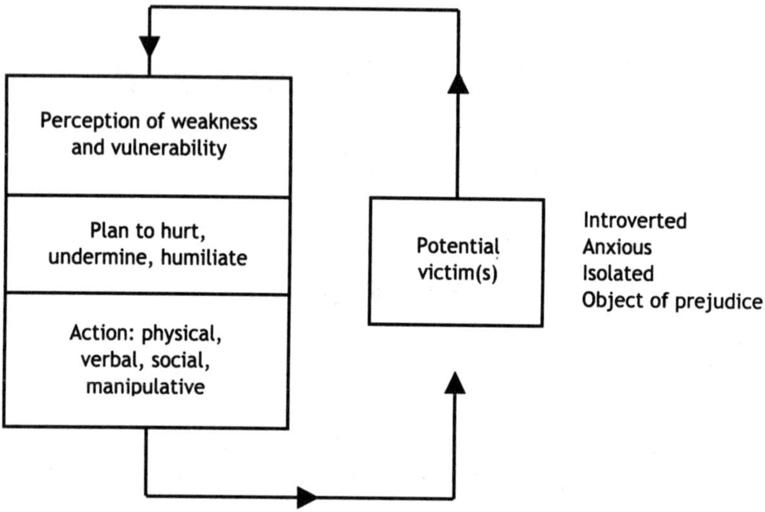

at the phenomena of bullying more closely, physical domination is not even a central feature of bullying at school. In my studies of bullying among Australian school children, based on survey results of over 38,000 children, it is verbal bullying and harassment that stand out as the most frequent form of personal abuse, followed by exclusion and social manipulation. Both boys and girls report being bullied mostly in these ways; physical threats and attacks, though more common among boys, are in fact relatively rare. Sadly, verbal and indirect forms of bullying are commonplace in schools – about one child in eight has reported being 'often' treated by peers in these ways (Rigby, 1997).

Hence it is quite misleading to assume that bullying at school is largely physical and experienced only by boys. As is the case of the workplace, it is the things that males and females say (or do not say) to hurt others rather than the physical blows they deliver that constitute the primary means of bullying.

The Process of Bullying at School

From studies of how bullying originates and develops it is possible to form a picture of the process of bullying. Figure 1.1 suggests the cycle of bullying normally begins when a child is seen as relatively weak and vulnerable to attack from others. We know from research that such children tend to be introverted, anxious, isolated and the objects of group prejudice.

Figure 1.2 The bully and the passive victim

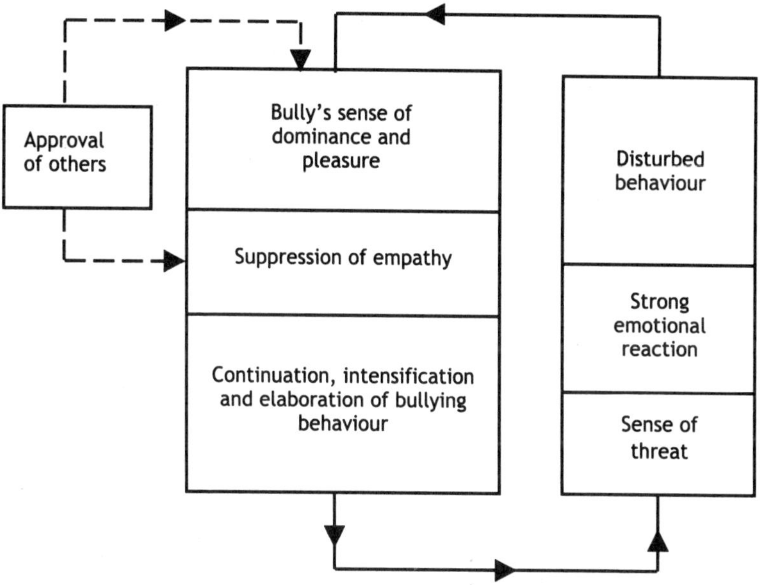

A more powerful child or group of children may decide to target potential victims and subject them to various forms of abuse. It may start with teasing and mild ridicule and go no further, but often it advances. Other children may join in. The victim's belongings may be moved or stolen; he or she may be verbally abused pushed and around or, in extreme cases, physically attacked. If the victim is passive and unresisting, the cycle may continue in the way suggested by Figure 1.2.

Such a victim typically feels threatened and fearful. If the victim shows signs of being disturbed or upset, this is evidence that the bullying is succeeding. The bully is then able to enjoy a pleasurable sense of dominance. If there is approval from others – friends and bystanders – any concern or empathy the bully may have for the plight of the victim quickly dissipates. It all seems like fun, and the cycle is likely to continue, the harassment to become more intense and the means more elaborate. We know that for many children the nightmare can go on for months and even years. Sometimes, of course, the victim may resist or take action to stop the bullying, as suggested in Figure 1.3 (see p 4).

The victim may seek (and sometimes find) ways of escaping or avoiding the tormentors, for instance, by keeping close to teachers or spending time in the school library. Alternatively, they may fight back,

Figure 1.3 The bully and the resistant victim

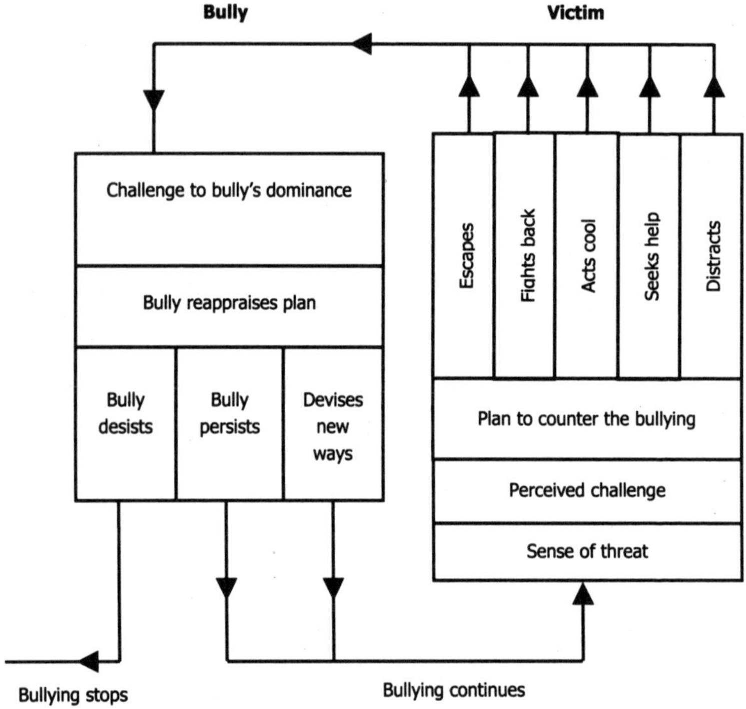

act assertively or perhaps even nonchalantly. But if the imbalance of power is too great and the bullying persistent, which it often is, such 'resistance' is likely to fail. Some children try to find others to help them, or, failing that, think up ways in which they can distract or amuse other children who might otherwise bully them. Do I exaggerate? If you ask Australian school children of all ages, as I have done, in anonymous questionnaires whether they personally could 'use some help' to stop being bullied, over one in three say that they could (Rigby, 1997).

Bullying at Work

Are there features of the schoolyard cycle that apply to bullying in the workplace? In my view there are many parallels. In any workplace, there are individuals who are particularly vulnerable to those who would bully them. There are also people who gain pleasure out of parading their 'superiority' at others' expense – often enough the very people who were bullies at school (see Farrington, 1993). There are those who appear to admire and approve of such bullying. As in the schoolyard, we see people struggling against the odds: avoiding or escaping when they can; asserting themselves when they dare; pretending they don't care, when they do; looking for help where it is hard to find; or pathetically trying to distract the bully when all else fails.

We should nevertheless recognise an important difference between the bullying of school children at school and the bullying of adults at work. Children are bullied for the most part by peers who have no formal organisational power over them, whereas adults are at least as likely to be bullied by managers and supervisors as by others who are lacking such authority. This being so, can we really equate the experience of being bullied at school with the experience of being bullied at work?

Studies in Germany by Zapf et al (1996) suggest that we can. Here are the items they identified as central to their five so-called 'mobbing' or bullying factors for assessing harassment in the workplace: (i) forcing somebody to carry out tasks that make them feel self-conscious; (ii) 'refusal to be talked to'; (iii) 'criticising a person's private life'; (iv) 'shouting at or cursing loudly at a person'; and (v) 'spreading rumours'. We know that to a lesser or greater degree children who bully others at school employ all of these tactics.

Of course, there are some benign workplaces, just as there are some relatively benign schools where bullying is not so common. In a way, this is an encouraging sign and should lead us to study social environments where people are more co-operative and supportive of each other. But we should also recognise that although it is fair to say that the adult who is being harassed at work may often have more resources and options than the child who is being victimised at school, the pressures on the adult in these times of downsizing and the constant threat of chronic unemployment can be equally overwhelming.

What Harm Does Bullying Do?

It is still not uncommon to find people who believe that bullying does no real harm. In the past we have had to rely on anecdotes and case studies of questionable value. But quite recently a number of studies have appeared that support the view that bullying does have harmful effects, through both bullying in schools and bullying in the workplace.

Correlational studies

For the most part these studies have been correlational, that is, they purport to show that relatively high levels of victimisation are associated with negative outcomes. As one would expect, research into the relationship between personal wellbeing and being bullied has been carried out more often in schools than in the workplace (see Rigby, 1998a, 1998b, 1999; Rigby and Slee, 1993, 1999; Salmon et al, 1998; Williams et al, 1996; Zubrick et al, 1997). Broadly these studies have established that among school children, relatively poor psychological health (as indicated by self-reported anxiety, depression, low self-esteem, suicidal ideation and a range of somatic symptoms) is reliably associated with being persistently bullied by peers at school.

Studies of the health correlates of bullying in the workplace are less common. Nevertheless, Zapf et al (1996) reported that respondents who had been identified through self-reports as frequently 'mobbed' or bullied at work were significantly more likely than others to report psychosomatic complaints and depression, and to have lower levels of self-esteem.

Knowing what we do about the effects of continual stress, it is extremely probable that being continually bullied or 'mobbed', whether at school or at work, induces anxiety and depression and weakens the immune system, resulting in higher levels of physical unwellness (see Cox, 1995). However, it is conceivable that the association between bullying and poor health derives from a different causal relationship. It is possible that being psychologically unwell typically elicits bullying behaviour from others.

Longitudinal studies

Longitudinal studies of the effects of bullying are needed to confirm beyond doubt that bullying is injurious to health. Thus far, three such studies have been conducted: two with primary school children in the USA (Egan and Perry, 1998: Kochenderfer and Ladd, 1996) and one with students attending a secondary school in Australia (Rigby, 1998c, 1999b). Both studies of American primary school children showed that the experience of being repeatedly bullied at school led directly to reduced levels of mental health. The Australian study examined possible health effects of bullying on secondary school students who reported relatively high levels of peer victimisation in the first two years of high school (Rigby, 1999b). In this study respondents included 43 boys and 35 girls who completed measures of physical and mental health in 1994 and again three years later. Analyses indicated that being victimised repeatedly, according to self-reports in 1994, significantly predicted poor mental and physical health in 1997, after controlling for: (i) level of reported health in 1994; (ii) degree of reported bullying in 1997; and (iii) the gender of the respondent. These studies strongly support the view that severe bullying can have both short- and long-term effects on the health of children at different levels of their schooling.

The extension of the effects of bullying on health into adult years has been suggested by several retrospective studies For example, Gilmartin (1987) reported that bullied children tended to avoid making close relations with others in later life; Dietz (1994) showed that depression among adults was associated with a history of peer victimisation at school; and Tritt and Duncan (1997) found that loneliness among college students was experienced significantly more often than average by those who had experienced childhood bullying.

Effects on performance

In focusing on the effects of bullying on the health of victims, we should not neglect the effects that being bullied can have on work performance. One index of such an effect is simply the school attendance record of children who have been bullied at school. We know that in Australia as many as 6% of schoolboys and 9% of schoolgirls report having missed days at school because of bullying (Rigby, 1996). We know, too, that the percentages of children who report having absented themselves from school because of bullying is considerably greater among those students who are bullied frequently, that is, at least once a week in the last 12 months. Among this group of frequently victimised children (about 15% of all school children), approximately one in four has reported staying away from school because of bullying (Rigby, 1996). To the effect on school performance due to absenteeism, one should add negative effects on the capacity of children to learn because of being in a state of anxiety and depression induced by the fear of being bullied.

Similar claims have been made regarding the effects on work performance of adults who experience chronic bullying in the workplace. In 1996 the Institute of Personnel and Development reported on the results of a survey conducted with over 1000 workers in the UK (see the website: http://www.successunlimited.co.uk/costs.htm). One in eight of the respondents claimed that they had been bullied at work during the last five years. Of these, some 72% said they had suffered work-related stress. Again, in estimating the effects of such stress we should take into account not only costs to employers through absences from work, but also effects on the work performance of large numbers of people who are continually being subjected to health-damaging harassment.

Dealing with bullying

I have argued that there are clear parallels between bullying in schools and bullying in the workplace. I also believe that studies of interventions to reduce bullying in schools are, in fact, more advanced than comparable studies in the workplace. What can we learn from schools?

The first thing is that the problem of bullying can be most effectively addressed when there is general agreement that: (i) it really does constitute a serious problem for a substantial number of people, and (ii) there are sensible and constructive things that can be done about it.

Some people do need to be convinced that there are people in their organisation whose lives are being seriously affected by a person or a group of people at work who continually mistreat or abuse them, in short, that there really are victims or potential victims of bullying in their workplace. In schools confirmation that this is in fact the case can readily be obtained, and has been obtained, by numerous schools that are willing to ask students the right questions. In Australia, the Peer Relations Questionnaire (PRQ) and the Peer Relations Assessment Questionnaires (PRAQs) have been widely used to obtain an accurate assessment of what kind of bullying occurs between children, how they feel about it and what they would like to see done about it (see the website: http://www.education.unisa.edu.au/bullying). There is no reason why similar questionnaires should not be employed to assess the quality of relations between people in the workplace.

Such knowledge as can be gained this way is, of course, a means to an end: to bring everyone to an appreciation of how people are regularly treating (or maltreating) each other and with what consequences. The next step is to formulate a suitable, and published, policy that is based on what has been discovered, and which is widely supported, not least of all by top management. Most schools in Australia do now have relevant policy statements to address bullying. In Queensland, having such a policy is mandatory, and resources are provided by the Education Department to encourage teachers to study the problem. As yet, few organisations have followed suit. They will do so, I think, when they appreciate not only the human misery induced by bullying, but also the economic costs that are incurred through an unmotivated and resentful workforce, avoidable absenteeism, and skilled and valuable personnel leaving to try their luck elsewhere.

Workplace management would do well to keep an eye on what some of the more progressive schools are doing. Whilst it is understandable to view bullying as an evil that needs to be crushed, increasingly schools are recognising that a policy that relies on 'beating the bully' is generally unwise and even counter-productive. This is not to say that there should be no sanctions applied when students repeatedly and cynically disregard the feelings of others. But the first step taken by schools when a case of bullying is presented should (I believe) invariably involve confronting the bully and sharing one's concern for the victim with the perpetrator, and inviting a responsible reaction.

This Method of Shared Concern devised by Anatol Pikas (see Rigby, 1996) has been remarkably successful in bringing about changes in the behaviour of most, though not all, children who bully. Seeking to crush bullying by penalties or 'consequences' is frequently unsuccessful because: (i) bullies are often adept at justifying their bullying behaviour (to themselves); (ii) they resent and react negatively towards condemnation; and (iii) they can very often 'get away with' subtle forms of bullying that can be profoundly hurtful and, in the 'legal' sense, virtually untouchable. Again, although there are occasions when the protection of others demands that the school or workplace suspend or dismiss unresponsive bullies, the use of positive and constructive means must be our main priority.

Finally, what we are learning from schools is that although initiating change through devising new policies and procedures must come from educational authorities, the reduction of bullying in schools can only occur on a big scale when there is an acceptance of responsibility by everyone in the school community, students as well as staff, for acting to discourage bullying, starting with oneself (see Petersen and Rigby, 1999). It is only when bystanders are prepared to put themselves in the place of the boy or girl or man or woman who is being bullied – whether at school or at work – and to voice their refusal to put up with it, that bullying will cease.

References

Cox, T (1995) 'Stress, Coping and Physical Health', in A Broome and S Llewelyn (eds), *Health Psychology: Process and Applications* (2nd edn). London: Singular Publication Group.

Dietz, B (1994) 'Effects on Subsequent Heterosexual Shyness and Depression of Peer Victimization at School'. Conference paper presented at the International Conference on Children's Peer Relations, 19–22 January, Institute of Social Research, University of South Australia, Adelaide.

Egan, S and Perry, D (1998) 'Does Low Self-Regard Invite Victimization?' 34(2) *Developmental Psychology* 299–309.

Farrington, D (1993) 'Understanding and Preventing Bullying', in M Tonry and N Morris (eds), *Crime and Justice* (vol 17). Chicago: University of Chicago Press, pp 381–458

Gilmartin, B (1987) 'Peer Group Antecedents of Severe Love-Shyness in Males' 55 *Journal of Personality* 467–89.

Kochenderfer, B and Ladd, G (1996) 'Peer Victimisation: Cause or Consequence of School Maladjustment' 67 *Child Development* 1305–17.

Petersen, L and Rigby, K (1999) 'Countering Bullying at an Australian Secondary School with Students as Helpers' 22 *Journal of Adolescence* 481–92.

Rigby, K (1996) *Bullying in Schools and What to Do about It.* Melbourne: Australian Council for Educational Research.

Rigby, K (1997) 'What Children Tell Us about Bullying in Schools' 22(2) *Children Australia* 28–34.

Rigby, K (1998a) 'The Relationship between Reported Health and Involvement in Bully/Victim Problems among Male and Female Secondary School Students' 3(4) *Journal of Health Psychology* 465–76.

Rigby, K (1998b) 'Suicidal Ideation and Bullying among Australian Secondary School Children' 15(1) *Australian Educational and Developmental Psychologist* 45–61.

Rigby, K (1998c) 'Peer Relations at School and the Health of Children' 17(1) *Youth Studies Australia* 13-17.

Rigby, K (1999) 'Peer Victimisation at School and the Health of Secondary Students' 22(2) *British Journal of Educational Psychology* 28–34.

Rigby, K (2000) 'Effects Of Peer Victimisation in Schools and Perceived Social Support on Adolescent Well-Being' 23 *Journal of Adolescence* 57–68.

Rigby, K and Slee, P (1993) 'Dimensions of Interpersonal Relations among Australian School Children and Their Implications for Psychological Well-Being' 133(1) *Journal of Social Psychology* 33–42.

Rigby, K and Slee, P (1999) 'Suicidal Ideation among Adolescent School Children, Involvement in Bully/Victim Problems and Perceived Low Social Support' 29 *Suicide and Life-Threatening Behavior* 119–130.

Salmon, G, Jones, A and Smith, D (1998) 'Bullying in School: Self-Reported Anxiety and Self-Esteem in Secondary School Children' 317 (7163) *British Medical Journal* 924–5.

Tritt, C and Duncan, RD (1997) 'The Relationship between Childhood Bullying and Young Adult Self-Esteem and Loneliness' 36 *Journal of Humanistic Education and Development* 35–44.

Williams, K, Chambers, M, Logan, S and Robinson, D (1996) 'Association of Common Health Symptoms with Bullying in Primary School Children' 313 *British Medical Journal* 17–19.

Zapf, D, Knorz, C and Kulla, M (1996) 'On the Relationship between Mobbing Factors and Job Content: The Social Work Environment and Health Outcomes' 5(2) *European Journal of Work and Organizational Psychology* 215–37.

Zubrick, S, Silburn, S, Gurrin, L, Teoh, H, Shepherd, C, Carlton, J and Lawrence, D (1997) *Western Australian Child Health Survey: Education, Health and Competence.* Perth: Australian Bureau of Statistics and Institute for Child Health Research.

Chapter 2

European Research on Bullying at Work

Dieter Zapf

This chapter starts with a short introduction that defines bullying and places it in a theoretical context. Some descriptive data on the frequency and duration of bullying is then presented. Finally, various causes of bullying are discussed and conclusions drawn.

Bullying research in Europe started in Sweden in the early 1980s and was introduced to German-speaking countries by Heinz Leymann (1993; 1996) at the beginning of the 1990s. Bullying, or mobbing as it is conceptualised in some European countries (Austria, Germany, Norway, Sweden, Switzerland and the Netherlands), signifies a severe form of harassing, badgering or tormenting people in organisations. Differences in meaning between mobbing and bullying are discussed below. Theoretically, this chapter contextualises bullying within research into conflict and stress.

Bullying as a Social Stressor

Bullying can be conceived of as a stressor in the context of stress research. The widely known transactional stress process model of Lazarus (Lazarus and Folkman, 1984), as applied in work psychology, provides a basis for the conceptualisation of bullying as a stressor. Lazarus's model suggests that a person perceives and appraises stressors according to the extent of threat and likelihood of coping. Reactions to these stressors may be short term and long term. Typically, several groups of stressors can be differentiated. There are physical, environmental, social and cognitive stressors. In terms of Lazarus's model, bullying can be identified as a severe social stressor at work, and can have severe health consequences for victims.

Although social stressors in organisations appear to be neglected in scientific research (Keashly et al, 1997; Zapf, 1999a), there is some empirical evidence concerning the importance of social stressors in comparison to other stressors in organisations. For example, a diary study by Schwartz and Stone (1993) found that 15% of the most stressful events of the day comprised negative emotional interactions with colleagues, supervisors or clients, and these were the second most frequent category recorded.

The basic characteristic of social stressors is that they arise within social relations at work. Social stressors, including bullying, occur as daily hassles, although bullying can assume greater severity as critical life events. Examples of more severe forms of bullying include the use of physical or sexual violence, or the removal of substantial involvement in decision-making, which may completely change the status of a person in the firm. Social stressors may arise more or less often. Leymann (1996) suggested that to qualify as bullying, negative behaviours should occur at least once a week for at least half a year. Social stressors can occur under both equal or unequal power structures. Whilst bullying can start with an equal power structure, after some time an unequal power structure will result and limit the resources of the victims to defend themselves. Finally, if social stressors occur in a department, almost everybody will be negatively affected after some time. Bullying, however, is targeted at a particular person. These considerations lead to the following definition of bullying or mobbing: bullying or mobbing occurs if somebody is harassed, offended, socially excluded or has to carry out humiliating tasks and the person concerned is in an inferior position. To call something bullying or mobbing, it must occur repeatedly (for example, at least once a week) and for a long time (for example, at least six months). It is not bullying or mobbing if it is a single event. It is also not bullying or mobbing when two equally strong parties are in conflict (cf Einarsen, 2000; Einarsen and Skogstad, 1996; Leymann, 1993; Zapf, 1999a).

Mobbing or Bullying? A Question of Perspective

Different perspectives on bullying within Europe are of interest. The British view tends to focus on the bully (Hoel et al, 1999; Rayner, 1997). For example, the influencing book of Andrea Adams (1992) is full of stories about bullies who typically are supervisors, and how they mistreat subordinates, individually or severally. Accordingly, a bully could be defined as someone who does this regularly, over a long period. Misuse of power, poor social skills and personality problems of the bully are frequently give as reasons bullying occurs.

On the other hand, "mobbing" research has always had a clear focus on the victim. Leymann's (1993, 1996) research demonstrated the potential for workplace conflicts to have severe health consequences. His findings challenged the view of many health professionals, such as doctors or psychologists, who were less inclined to attribute their patient's ill-health to factors such as mobbing. As a strong advocate for victims, Leymann rejected suggestions they could be responsible for their own fate. On the other hand, he also did not speculate on the personality of the perpetrators as is often done in bullying research. Rather, Leymann attributed responsibility for mobbing to the organisation.

Research findings also vary according to these perspectives. Comparison of the percentages of supervisors, colleagues and subordinates reported as bullies in various studies in Europe (see Zapf, 1999a) indicates supervisors were involved in more than 50% of all cases. Often, they were involved in more than 70% of cases. These findings suggest that, in many respects, bullying is a leadership problem. In most studies bullying of colleagues is equally frequent, although less so in the UK. There, the percentage of colleagues involved in bullying is much lower compared to that in other European countries (Rayner, 1997). These differences suggest that bullying and mobbing have different meanings.

A person's choice of terms and definitions may reflect their intention. For example, some prefer to use looser criteria to allow minor conflicts to be considered as bullying, and to underscore the harmfulness of conflicts at work, which might otherwise be ignored. Use of the term 'bullying' also seems to imply more a bully-focused definition. It expresses an interest in the behaviour of the perpetrator and in showing there are leadership and management problems that can have dire consequences. This focus then leads to an emphasis on remedies such as personnel development.

Finally, use of the term mobbing is evident in victim-focused definitions that reflect an interest in the health problems of the victims. These definitions attribute health problems and psychological disorders, such as post-traumatic stress disorders, to mobbing. They do not attribute these psychological disorders to disposition or premorbidity (Leymann and Gustafsson, 1996). Those advocating this position take issue with medical and psychological misdiagnoses of health professionals. Their focus is commonly on developing psychotherapeutic remedies.

Frequency and Duration of Bullying

Frequency

One might well argue that whilst bullying may occur, its occurrence is so seldom as to warrant little attention. This viewpoint has contributed to lack of attention to the problem of bullying by employers in Germany, and has been a factor in difficulties in developing reliable measures of the frequency of bullying. The frequency of bullying also depends very much on how it is measured (cf Hoel et al, 1999). The measures, again, are influenced by the general understanding of what bullying is.

Some researchers have developed questionnaires, the responses to which are subjected to cut-off points that produce frequencies of bullying ranging from 10% to 17% (for example, Björkqvist et al, 1994). Others have used the Leymann Inventory of Psychological Terrorisation (LIPT) (Leymann, 1996). To be considered a victim of bullying, according to the LIPT criteria, a respondent should have experienced at least one of 45 negative behaviours, at least once a week, for at least six months. The LIPT questionnaire commonly produces frequencies of bullying from 3% to 7% of respondents (Zapf, 1999a). Others researchers have directly asked: 'Have you been bullied during the last six months?' Typically, this approach leads to between 10% and 25% reporting they have been bullied, since infrequent, minor negative actions tend to be included. Another strategy is to give a precise definition of what bullying is, for example, the definition given above. Commonly, between 1% and 4% of respondents report they have been bullied within the terms of such a definition (for example, Einarsen and Skogstad, 1996).

There is, of course, a relation between the researcher's interests, their approach to measuring bullying, and frequencies of bullying reported. For example, Swedish, Norwegian, Austrian and German researchers tend to use a fairly strict definition of bullying, whereas in the UK the definitions are much looser. An overview of European studies that measure more in terms of the above definition indicates that between 1% and 4% of respondents experience serious bullying (Zapf, 1999a). While these levels of bullying can be neglected by employers and by employees' associations, they should not be. The findings also imply that bullying contributes to high levels of social stress more often than these results suggest.

Duration

In many European countries, even minor everyday conflicts and arguments are called mobbing or bullying. Therefore, the duration of bullying is an important criterion to differentiate between everyday conflicts in organisations and bullying. The long duration of organisational conflicts classified as bullying has been noted in a number of European studies. In the large representative samples in Sweden (Leymann, 1996) and Norway (Einarsen and Skogstad, 1996), the average duration of a bullying case was 15 and 18 months respectively. In other studies where victims of bullying were systematically approached, the average duration was much higher, with a mean of more than three years (for example, Leymann and Gustafsson, 1996; Zapf, 1999a). This difference is due to the method of sampling. Location of victims through advisory agencies and self-help groups leads to self selection of those who have experienced more severe bullying in a sample. In any case, the above studies indicate bullying is not a short episode, but a process of 'wearing down', mostly lasting much longer than a year.

What Causes Bullying?

This question generates heated discussions. On the one side, some media and employers, supported by many doctors and clinical psychologists, do not believe that severe symptoms observed in victims of bullying can be attributed to workplace factors. Instead, they diagnose the experience of the victim in terms of 'complaining' or 'general anxiety disorder', and refer to a substantial body of case evidence in justifying these claims. They suggest these disorders existed before the bullying process began and attribute the reason for the bullying to them, effectively blaming victims of bullying for their being bullied.

On the other side, Heinz Leymann's seminal research into mobbing provides a point of reference for those who attribute victims' experiences to work environment factors. This side claims that organisational problems, particularly those related to the organisation of work and leadership, are the cause of mobbing (Leymann, 1993, 1996). However, there is insufficient research to support a definitive answer to this question. Reasons for differences are predominantly methodological. The studies are all cross-sectional and many of them lack the use of established instruments to measure the work environment and leadership behaviour (Zapf, 1999b).

Figure 2.1 (p 17) presents a more fluid model of relations between the causes and consequences of bullying. The model addresses the problem of the direction of causes, as a key difficulty in bullying research. Four potential causes of bullying are shown on the left hand side of the figure. They are the organisation, the perpetrator (the bully), the social group at work, and the victim of bullying. The perpetrator usually overlaps with the social group and the organisation, for example, in the case of a supervisor. As the model suggests, causal paths do not just go from left to right. For example, whilst organisational factors may lead to observable bullying behaviour and to health complaints in the victim, one could also assume that anxious, depressive or obsessive behaviour produces a negative reaction in the group, resulting in bullying after some time. In turn, bullying could degrade the social climate and undermine social support with the effect of weakening the information flow. As a consequence, job stressors such as uncertainty about goal achievement and organisational problems may arise (Zapf, 1999b).

Personal causes of bullying: the perpetrator

In a study by Zapf (1999b), the most frequent reason victims gave for their being bullied was, 'they wanted to push me out of the company'. The second reason most commonly given located responsibility for the bullying with a particular person. In other studies, many victims considered envy as a core reason behind bullying (Björkqvist et al, 1994; Einarsen et al, 1994; Vartia, 1996). Other reasons given for bullying included a weak superior, competition for tasks, status or advancement, or competition for the supervisor's favour (Einarsen, 2000).

Of course, such findings need to be qualified in terms of the potential for attribution errors. For example, causes of bullying may be more easily attributed to a person than to less visible circumstances. Thus, causes originating in organisational circumstances or in the social system could in some cases be attributed to particular persons.

Organisational causes of bullying

An interesting indicator of ways that organisational factors contribute to bullying arises in the interpretation of findings from various European studies. These studies converge in finding that bullying generally occurs less often among factory workers and more often among office workers and managers. Furthermore, the evidence suggests there is more bullying among teachers and in the social and health care service, in public administration and in the banking and insurance sector (Einarsen and Skogstad, 1996; Leymann, 1993; Zapf, 1999a).

Reports of higher levels of bullying in these sectors could be related to their more difficult career dynamics. Career pathways may either not exist, as in many parts of the social and health services, or be less influenced by achievement and depend more on seniority, time in the organisation and relationships. These factors may well increase micropolitics at work, which, coupled with poor conflict resolution, increase the level of bullying reported among these occupations and industry sectors. A second related reason may be that the work performance in these occupations and sectors may be more difficult to appraise. For example, it is much easier to assess objectively whether the work of an assembly line worker was well done compared with that of a teacher or a doctor. These difficulties could also be a source of potential conflicts. Bullying

Figure 2.1 Causes and consequences of bullying at work (Zapf, 1999b: 71)

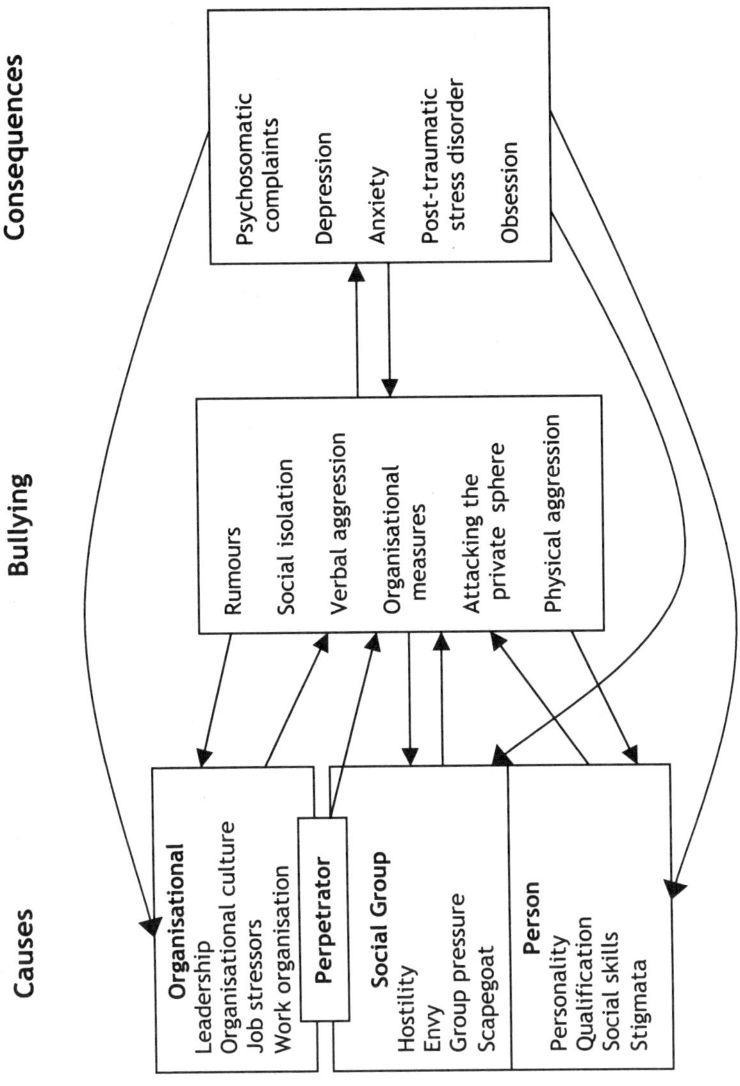

through the use of organisational procedures, such as ongoing criticism of a person's work or giving someone humiliating or senseless tasks, may also be less accountable in these circumstances (Zapf et al, 1996).

A third reason, and perhaps the most important, for higher reports of bullying by office workers and managers than by factory workers is related to the level of job skills and tenure. Less skilled factory workers who can find jobs elsewhere may simply quit in the face of escalating conflicts. However, public sector employees may endure bullying in the interests of job security, as indicated by their persistence in jobs commonly earning less than those in private industry. The extent to which bullying is reported may also relate to different levels of protection of workers' rights and expectations regarding job tenure between countries. For example, bullying research started in those countries that have the most developed laws to protect workers' rights, namely Sweden and Norway. In contrast, in the USA where workers seem more attuned to flexibility and job changes, and where there are fewer constraints on sacking a person, bullying research is just gaining momentum (Keashly et al, 1997). In this sense, bullying emerges as the 'dark side' of job security.

The reasons why conflicts escalate into bullying may also be derived from the probability of conflicts and the capacity to resolve them in an organisation. The probability that a conflict might not be resolved but will escalate is likely to be higher in organisations with a higher probability of conflicts in the first instance. For example, work may be organised in a way that is predisposed to conflict. Certain practices may make co-operation more difficult, such as unclear or contradicting goals that induce rivalry. Characteristics such as these, coupled with intense time pressures that leave little time for conflict management, may lead to higher risks of bullying. Several studies support such a scenario (Einarsen et al, 1994; Vartia, 1996; Zapf, 1999b).

Characteristics of the victim and their social group

Responses to several items in a study by Zapf (1999b) suggest that reasons for bullying may relate to characteristics of the victim, at least partly. Although, interestingly, these responses were less frequent, occurring among 37% of the victims, with 63% not associating them with their experience of bullying. However, the cause and responsibility for bullying need to be distinguished. For example, while a cause may be located 'in the victim', responsibility may lie within a social group that is unable to integrate a person who may be different in some respect. Notably, only 2% of those experiencing bullying in this study 'admitted' their performance was below average.

An indication that bullying may be a property of the social system is also given by studies relating bullying to organisational entry. Studies completed in Germany and Switzerland found that a third of victims experienced bullying within the first six months of employment, as against a quarter who had been in their job for more than five years (von Holzen-Beusch et al, 1999; Knorz and Zapf, 1996). In a study in the UK that supports these findings, Rayner (1997) found that 51% of victims attributed experiences of bullying to a recent job changes, 31% to a change of the supervisor, and 9% to a change of ownership. These findings suggest that better management of personnel changes and organisational entry may well reduce related incidences of bullying.

As group psychology suggests, those who are outsiders in some respect and differ from the rest of the group risk being made a scapegoat (Thylefors, 1987). Differences perceived by victims between themselves and others were profiled in a study by Zapf and Bühler (1998). The researchers developed a list of items of possible difference with professionals and victims, and sought responses in terms of 'I am more attractive', 'I am more accurate' and so on. The results showed that, in comparison to a control group, victims of bullying saw themselves more often as different from their colleagues in several respects. Most interestingly, the findings revealed there were heterogeneous groups of victims. One group corresponded to what most people would expect, being low in social competencies, bad conflict managers, and unassertive and weak personalities. These characteristics overlap with those that describe victims of school bullying (Einarsen, 2000).

However, another group of victims described themselves as more achievement-oriented and more conscientious than their colleagues. They were certainly not the least efficient employees in the organisation, but were not very high in empathy and clashed with their work group norms. Recently, two cases of suicide by young police women in Germany fit this schema. They wanted to be very good police officers and to give their best, but on occasions they departed from work group norms as a way of improving the quality of their work life in the face of difficulties experienced with male colleagues. For example, they sometimes played cards while on duty. Their 'outsider' behaviour was perceived as a strong threat to the group by male colleagues who valued mutual reliability. As a consequence, the police women were bullied to the extent they committed suicide.

High levels of neuroticism have also been found among victims of bullying in studies completed in a number of countries (for example, Einarsen et al, 1994; Gemzøe Mikkelsen and Einarsen, 1999; Vartia, 1996; Zapf, 1999b). Neurotic individuals tend to show high levels of emotional instability, anxiety and depressive symptoms. However, the possibility that the victims' symptoms were a consequence of bullying, rather than a cause, cannot be disregarded, although it is unlikely this was so in all cases.

Conclusion

Whilst further research into the causes of mobbing is required, existing empirical data suggests there are many, probably often multiple, causes of bullying. These causes have been identified in the organisation, the perpetrator, the social system and the victim. Locating the causes of bullying in just one or other of these situations or actors risks being misleading. Cases of bullying can be markedly different, and the conditions in each case need to be carefully considered.

Professionals need to be mindful that the services they provide to victims of bullying may be sought by persons with different dispositions and situations, which lead them to choose particular remedies. Psychiatrists and psychotherapists commonly treat causes of bullying they locate in the victim, and those seeking their services may self-select in these terms. However, they may be consulted by victims of bullying that stems from organisational factors or a particular perpetrator, and these victims cope with the problem themselves. For example, they may consult their family doctor and feel most relieved when the bullying has ceased, and not pursue psycho-therapeutic remedies. On the other hand, victims who fight for their rights, to the point of being 'overachievers', have also been identified. They may seek out assistance from trade union representatives and lawyers in pursuing their legal rights for months, even years. Given these complexities, personal experiences of bullying at work should not be over-generalised.

Evidence suggests that bullying is too frequent to ignore. However, the heterogeneous nature of bullying and its various causes need to be appreciated. Measures for intervention and prevention need to account for different professional understandings, characteristics of victims and perpetrators, and social group and organisational factors that come into play in cases of bullying. Specific measures are needed, since there are no general solutions. The problem remains that professionals involved in helping victims of bullying tend to be approached by those whose dispositions and situations align with the understandings of bullying and remedies offered by those professionals. There is also the danger that professionals develop and adhere to one-sided views of the nature of bullying. In the interests of overcoming bullying, the dialogue across disciplines is, therefore, important.

References

Adams, A (1992) *Bullying at Work: How to Confront and Overcome It.* London: Virago Press.

Björkqvist, K, Österman, K and Hjelt-Bäck, M (1994) 'Aggression among University Employees' 20 *Aggressive Behaviour* 173–84.

Einarsen, S (2000) 'Bullying and Harassment at Work: A Review of the Scandinavian Approach' 5 *Aggression and Violent Behaviour* 379–401.

Einarsen, S and Skogstad, A (1996) 'Bullying at Work: Epidemiological Findings in Public and Private Organizations' 5 *European Journal of Work and Organizational Psychology* 185–202.

Einarsen, S, Raknes, BI and Matthiesen, S (1994) 'Bullying and Harassment at Work and Their Relationships to Work Environment Quality: An Exploratory Study' 4(4) *European Journal of Work and Organizational Psychology* 381–401.

Gemzøe Mikkelsen, E and Einarsen, S (1999) 'The Role of Victim Personality in Workplace Bullying'. Unpublished MS, Institute of Psychology, Risskov, Denmark.

Hoel, H, Rayner, C and Cooper, CL (1999) 'Workplace Bullying', in CL Cooper and IT Robertson (eds), *International Review of Industrial and Organizational Psychology* (vol 14). Chichester: Wiley.

von Holzen-Beusch, E, Zapf, D and Schallberger, U (1999) '*Warum Mobbingopfer ihre Arbeitsstelle nicht wechseln*' [Why the Victims of Bullying do not Change Their Job]. Unpublished MS, Department of Psychology, University of Zurich, Switzerland.

Keashly, L, Hunter, S and Harvey, S (1997) 'Abusive Interaction and Role State Stressors: The Relative Impact on Student Residence Assistant Stress and Work Attitudes' 11 *Work and Stress* 175–85.

Knorz, C and Zapf, D (1996) '*Mobbing: eine extreme Form sozialer Stressoren am Arbeitsplatz*' [Mobbing: An Extreme Form of Social Stressors at Work] 40 *Zeitschrift für Arbeits- und Organisationspsychologie* 12–21.

Lazarus, RS and Folkman, S (1984) *Stress, Appraisal and Coping.* New York: Springer.

Leymann, H (1993) *Mobbing: Psychoterror am Arbeitsplatz und wie man sich dagegen wehren kann* [Mobbing: Psychoterror at Work and How to Defend Oneself]. Reinbeck: Rowohlt.

Leymann, H (1996) 'The Content and Development of Mobbing at Work' 5(2) *European Journal of Work and Organizational Psychology* 165–84.

Leymann, H and Gustafsson, A (1996) 'Mobbing at Work and the Development of Post-traumatic Stress Disorders' 5(2) *European Journal of Work and Organizational Psychology* 251–76.

Rayner, C (1997) 'The Incidence of Workplace Bullying' 7 *Journal of Community and Applied Social Psychology* 199–208.

Schwartz, JE and Stone, AA (1993) 'Coping with Daily Work Problems: Contributions of Problem Content, Appraisals, and Person Factors' 7 *Work and Stress* 47–62.

Thylefors, I (1987) *Syndabockar: Om utstötning och mobbning i arbetslivet* [Scapegoats: On Expulsion and Bullying in Working Life]. Stockholm: Natur och Kulture.

Vartia, M (1996) 'The Sources of Bullying: Psychological Work Environment and Organizational Climate' 5(2) *European Journal of Work and Organizational Psychology* 203–14.

Zapf, D (1999a) '*Mobbing in Organisationen: Ein Überblick zum Stand der Forschung*' [Mobbing in Organisations: A State of the Art of Research Review] 43 *Zeitschrift für Arbeits- und Organisationspsychologie* 1–25.

Zapf, D (1999b) 'Organizational, Work Group Related and Personal Causes of Mobbing/Bullying at Work' 20 *International Journal of Manpower* 70–85.

Zapf, D and Bühler, K (1998) 'Exclusion and Stigmatization at Work'. Unpublished manuscript, Department of Psychology, Goethe-University, Frankfurt.

Zapf, D, Knorz, C and Kulla, M (1996) 'On the Relationship between Mobbing Factors, and Job Content, the Social Work Environment and Health Outcomes' 5(2) *European Journal of Work and Organizational Psychology* 215–37.

Chapter 3

Bullying in the Helping Professions

Jane Rylance

Each profession is characterised by stereotypes that shape the perceptions of those who work within them. These perceptions can restrain the acknowledgment and addressing of behaviours that differ from the dominant images. Focusing more specifically on social service workers whose major 'tool' is that of human relations skills for the enhancement of people's wellbeing, it is evident that a variety of expectations exist around the people they are and how they should behave. Thus, in their 'helping' roles, they are commonly stereotyped in terms of being caring, sensitive and respectful. This chapter reports the findings of a survey on bullying, taken from a sample of workers in the helping professions. Furthermore, it examines the incongruence of this behaviour with the ways in which these professionals and their work are commonly constructed.

The last decade has witnessed a proliferation of anecdotal and empirical evidence surrounding the phenomenon of workplace bullying or abuse (see Einarsen (2000a) and Hoel et al (1999) for summaries of this literature). The foci of these have been on causal factors, consequences and descriptive dimensions of the bullying experience.

These have occurred across different professions, but have not specifically focused on workers within the social services sector. Exploring some of the dominant themes in the literature about those in the social service professions, and contrasting these themes with some of the findings in a study examining workplace bullying and abuse among social service workers, this chapter will show that behaviours occur within these professions that are clearly incongruent. Furthermore, the findings challenge some of the dominant role constructions of the client–helper relationship, by suggesting that clients may be the target of some of these behaviours by workers.

Definition of Workplace Bullying

Definitions of workplace bullying or abuse are complicated by the growing awareness of the heterogeneity of the experience in terms of its nature and its causal factors (see Zapf, Chapter 2, this volume). Recent discussion has also ensued regarding the issues of 'objectivity' versus 'subjectivity' in defining and researching the phenomenon (for example, Einarsen, 2000a; Hoel et al, 1999). In fact, the growing awareness of the multi-dimensionality of the phenomenon of workplace bullying heralds a shift in thinking and research. The importance of subjectivity as being essential to any understandings of bullying has also been acknowledged (Einarsen, 2000a; Hoel et al, 1999). The definition adopted here considers the inherent dilemmas of purely 'objective' or 'subjective' stances and has opted for an approach encompassing the important subjective elements, whilst still ensuring the inclusion of basic criteria that distinguish the experience from other phenomena. Thus, bullying occurs when 'someone persistently, over a period of time, perceives himself to be on the receiving end of negative actions from one or several others, in a situation where the one at the receiving end has difficulties defending against these actions' (Einarsen, 2000b).

Stereotypes of Helping

Two major stereotypes emerge from the literature about the helping professions, which may contribute to abusive behaviour appearing as 'incongruent'. The first relates to the construction of workers. The second relates to the construction of the worker–client interaction. Thus, in exploring the first of these two images, it can be noted that an important expectation of workers in this field is that they show care and respect to the users of the services they provide. A number of authors have highlighted that the relationship between the 'helper' and the 'helped' is at the core of social service work (Braye and Preston-Shoot, 1995; Brill, 1995; Germain and Gitterman, 1996; O'Connor et al, 1998; Rothman, 1994; Sheafor et al, 1997; Taylor and Devine, 1993). Central to this interaction is the value of respect for the dignity of each person (Braye and Preston-Shoot, 1995; Germain and Gitterman, 1996; O'Connor et al, 1998). The code of ethics for the Australian Institute of Welfare and Community Workers, for example, reminds professionals of their obligation to 'treat clients with respect [and] to promote maximum self-worth and dignity' in their work with clients. This code also alerts workers to their obligations of providing 'loyalty and support to colleagues' and respecting other practitioners' 'skills and conceptual abilities'.

Some of the literature on burnout among the helping professions exemplifies these qualities further. Thus, concepts used to describe those who enter these professions refer to their level of 'caring' towards others. Pines et al (1980: 51–2) refer to social service workers as being 'particularly sensitive towards others', having 'great empathy to the suffering of others' and being 'essentially humanitarian'. Maslach (1982) has discussed the 'cost of caring'. Together, the expectations of worker behaviour, the codes of conduct and the burnout literature portray these workers as being 'extra' caring, respectful and sensitive individuals. In addition, people in these occupations can risk emotional and physical exhaustion (Maslach, 1982: 73) due to their interactions with clients, which contribute to burnout.

Furthermore, descriptions of the roles of many occupations in the helping professions are highly value-based. A number of authors have focused on the importance of values as guiding principles for social service work (Braye and Preston-Shoot, 1995; Germain and Gitterman, 1996; O'Connor et al, 1998). Scheafor et al (1997: 16), for example, encourage future social workers to consider if there exists a 'good fit between [their] personal beliefs, values, and needs and the values and demands of the social work profession'. In short, they suggest that social workers seek social justice, which is described, using Barker's definition (1995: 354), as 'an ideal condition in which all members of society have the same rights, protection, opportunities, obligations and social benefits'.

Social service work is value driven. Values such as those of client self-determination and empowerment are examples of important goals in this work (O'Connor et al, 1998). The Australian Association of Social Workers' Code of Ethics, for example, reminds workers of the importance of a commitment to social justice and client self-determination. A strong value base is important for all professions. Arguably, however, the strong value base underpinning the work of many social service workers assists in creating the stereotype of these workers as being almost beyond reproach in terms of their behaviour.

In examining the construction of the worker–client relationship, it is recognised that central to the 'helping' interaction is the demarcation between the 'helper' and the 'helped'. For it is the 'helper' who is somehow more 'able' or more 'resourced' to assist the sometimes less 'resourced' or more vulnerable client. In fact, there is a considerable body of literature that recognises the power held by those in the helping professions in the worker–client relationship. These discussions assist in establishing a demarcation between the 'helper' and the 'helped'. Thus, O'Connor and his colleagues (1998) have highlighted a source of power in the helping relationship that derives from the authority of knowledge.

Harris (1997: 30) has suggested that those in the helping professions such as social workers 'usually work with people who are relatively powerless'. Hasenfeld (1992: 260) has shown that professional social workers 'rely on the power of expertise, which is derived from their access to and command of specialized knowledge'. In addition, they also use 'referent power or persuasion, which emanates from their interpersonal skills, particularly their ability to develop empathy, trust and rapport with the client'.

The centrality of this interaction in the work of those in the helping professions creates a picture of these professionals as being more resourced or able than the person to whom they provide services. A clear boundary is placed between the two that highlights difference and establishes one as being more able than the other. Furthermore, the characteristics of this relationship, coupled with the codes of ethics of various social service professions, reinforce the image that such workers possess a high level of respect for the dignity of all people interacting with them.

Violence and Abuse from Service Users

There is also a body of literature that focuses on violence and abuse from the service users towards workers in the helping professions (Bowie, 1989; Brady, 1993; Brennan, 1996; Newhill, 1996; Rey, 1996). This literature emphasises the risks faced by workers within the helping professions. Thus, it attempts to acknowledge these risks, to research the incidence of violence, to highlight the impact of this violent behaviour and to discuss ways of preventing it and coping with it. This body of literature assists in establishing the notion of service users as being a potential danger to the emotional and physical safety of social service workers. Thus, it is the service users who are potentially abusive and violent to those in the helping occupations. A silence exists around similar behaviours occurring in the opposite direction.

Thus, these bodies of literature establish a demarcation between the behaviours of workers and the behaviours of clients. They present a clear boundary between the 'helper' and the 'helped'. They construct an image of social service workers as being caring people who may risk emotional and physical health as a result of working with clients. What these stereotypes mask, however, is an acknowledgment of the abusive and destructive behaviours of workers towards their colleagues in the helping professions. Furthermore, these constructs mask the fact that workers in this sector can be abusive to clients. The 'caring' image or stereotype make such behaviours among these workers seem 'incongruent'. They clearly do not allow for a recognition that all people are capable of behaving abusively and that the 'great divide' between 'helper' and 'helped' may not actually be so great.

Findings of a Study of Bullying in the Helping Professions

The following results are from a research project conducted at the School of Social Work and Social Policy at the University of Queensland. These results show, firstly, that workers in the helping professions can behave abusively to each other. Secondly, they highlight the fact that such abusive behaviour from fellow colleagues is an issue that requires addressing *in addition* to abuse from clients. Thirdly, they suggest that abuse in organisations employing social service workers could be detrimental to clients. Thus, of those employees who identified abuse by colleagues, many also identified similar behaviours by workers towards service users. These results challenge some of the dominant stereotypes in the literature on the helping professions.

Sample description

Surveys were sent to a variety of organisational and worker representative bodies across Queensland. These were the Australian Association of Social Workers, the Queensland Council of Social Services, the Social and Community Services Division of the Australian Services Union, the Family Support Officers of the Department of Families, Youth and Community Care who were members of the State Public Services Federation of Queensland, the Child and Family Welfare Association of Queensland, and the Queensland Association of Family Therapy. In addition, a number of surveys were also sent to various departments across all the health regions in Queensland.

A definition of a social service worker was provided as 'someone whose major work "tools" are human relations skills for the purpose of enhancing people's wellbeing (for example, social workers, psychologists, welfare workers, counsellors, domestic violence workers, support workers, resource workers, managers and co-ordinators of programs that deliver social services, community development officers, mental health workers)'.

Four hundred and sixty-one surveys were received, but one was unusable, one very late and the other five did not fit the definition of social service worker. The response rate was 17.0%; 83.3% of respondents were women, 16.7% men, and 94.7% of respondents were currently employed in the social services sector. These figures are representative of the general gender breakdown within the social services sector. Table 3.1 outlines a breakdown of the sectors within which respondents currently worked.

Table 3.1 Employment sectors of respondents (n=454)

Not-for Profit Community Sector	Government Sector	For-profit Sector	Private Practice/ Consultancy
41%	51.3%	1.3%	1.1%

The majority of the respondents had social work qualifications, with the remaining respondents having other relevant qualifications in the welfare or clinical area. Qualifications of respondents are summarised in Table 3.2.

Table 3.2 Qualifications of respondents (n=454)

Social work	Degree in social sciences	Psychology	Diploma/ certificate in welfare	Other degrees related to social services	None
48%	5.7%	9.3%	7.9%	18.3%	8.1%

Experiences of workplace abuse

The first section of the survey sought worker perceptions as to what constitutes and causes workplace abuse. This has been argued by Einarsen (2000a) as an important new area for research. These findings will not be reported here. Respondents were also provided with a definition of workplace bullying and then asked whether they had experienced the phenomenon. In this second section of the survey, questions about the dimensions of these experiences were also asked. These findings will be reported below.

The majority of the 454 respondents reported having experienced workplace abuse at some stage of their careers. Table 3.3 (see p 29) outlines the percentages and numbers of those who reported experiencing workplace abuse (WA) and those who reported that they did not experience this phenomenon.

Workers who had experienced abuse were asked to identify the number of organisations in which it had occurred. Of the 339 respondents, 58.4% (198 respondents) had experienced it in just one organisation, while 30.1% (102 respondents) had experienced such incidents in two organisations. Thus, 88.5% (300 respondents) had experienced it in only one or two organisations.

Table 3.3 Respondents who experienced workplace abuse (WA) (n=454)

Have experienced WA		Have not experienced WA but have observed WA		Have neither experienced WA nor observed WA	
%	No of Respondents	%	No of Respondents	%	No of Respondents
74.7	339	15.6	71	9.7	44

Those who identified themselves as having been subject to this phenomenon were asked to identify specific behaviours. This question produced qualitative data. Most workers said they had experienced a variety of behaviours directed towards them. An analysis of the variety of reported behaviours allowed for a categorisation into five sub-sets. These are:

(1) using organisational measures to target the worker (for example, limiting opportunities for basic worker entitlements; deliberately overloading the individual with work; unexplained job changes; tampering with work areas; micro-management);
(2) using direct 'attacks' to target the worker (for example, critical comments; put-downs; verbal abuse; sexual harassment; physical violence; threats to job security);
(3) using the social system to target the worker (for example, gossip; isolation; scapegoating);
(4) using a dominating, dismissive attitude or manner (ignoring the worker; passive/aggressive behaviour towards staff; dismissing staff concerns regarding abuse);
(5) organisational abuse (for example, organisational change with no support; poor pay; poor working conditions).

Interestingly, the last category is really a set of other work-related issues outside bullying, as it is usually represented in the literature. Nevertheless, some respondents perceived these dimensions as constituting the phenomena. The most commonly experienced behaviours were constant denigrating comments about professional abilities or about the person, with 67.6% (229 respondents) reporting that these behaviours had been directed towards them. This was followed by 38.9% (132 respondents) reporting 'verbal abuse' or screaming being directed towards them. Other commonly experienced behaviours were intimidating body language and actions (27.4% or 93 respondents), slanderous gossip (23.3% or 78 respondents), isolation (23% or 77 respondents), and impeding the performance of work, and threats to job security (21.8% or 74 respondents for each).

Client-to-worker versus worker-to-worker abuse

All respondents were presented with a five-point Likert scale (1932), where they were asked to identify the extent to which they had experienced abusive behaviours from people within the organisation and clients of the organisation. The scale ranged from 'never' to 'frequently'. When comparing the highest levels of abuse ('often' or 'frequently') from workers and from clients, the majority of respondents reported experiencing greater levels of abuse from people within their organisation than from service users. These responses are summarised in Table 3.4 below.

Table 3.4 Experience of abuse from clients compared with people in the organisation (n=454)

'Often' or 'frequently' experienced abuse from clients		'Often' or 'frequently' experienced abuse from people within the organisation	
%	No of Respondents	%	No of Respondents
12.1	54	24.4	110

What this highlights is that although abuse from clients is an issue for workers in the helping professions, so too is treatment by fellow colleagues. These figures suggest that some workers perceive there to be greater levels of abuse by other workers than by service users.

Abusive behaviour towards service users

Of those who had experienced workplace abuse, 85.3% (289) said the person or people engaged in the abusive behaviours towards them had contact with clients, and 43.6% (126) of these respondents said they had witnessed abusive or violent behaviour towards clients by the colleagues who were abusive to them. In addition to this, 4.1% (12 respondents) said the abusive behaviours directly involving the clients included being criticised or yelled at in front of clients, or other colleagues gossiping to clients about the specific worker.

What these figures suggest is that where there is workplace bullying or abuse as identified by workers, service users may experience these behaviours indirectly and directly. Thus:

(1) service users–clients can be involved in abusive incidents aimed at workers; and,

(2) service users–clients can be directly subject to abusive behaviour by the people identified as being abusive to the workers.

Discussion

This study is not representative and so caution is required in extrapolating from the results. Furthermore, the validity issues concerning self-labelling and self-reporting have also been recognised (Hoel et al, 1999). Nevertheless, these results challenge some of the dominant stereotypes of social service workers. Firstly, they indicate that workers in these professions do not always treat each other with respect and dignity. Secondly, they suggest that abusive treatment by workers is a concern, as is abuse by clients. Thirdly, they highlight that, in addition to clients being abusive to workers, service users can experience similar behaviours by workers. These figures suggest that where this phenomenon exists between workers in the helping professions, there is the potential for clients to be involved, either directly or indirectly.

The findings therefore indicate that the images of the 'caring', 'empathic' person who chooses to work in the helping professions needs to be balanced with a recognition that some workers can also behave abusively. Alongside the valuable and respectful work done by many in these professions, inappropriate and destructive behaviour also exists. Workers are capable of acting abusively, in ways that some service users are reported to operate. People in the helping professions are often working with clients who are dealing with their own experiences of abuse, or who also operate abusively themselves. It could be argued, therefore, that those in these occupations may not be as different from their client groups as the 'helping–helped' dynamic can portray.

Given that the study findings implicate both service workers and users in workplace abuse, and that there is a growing body of literature reporting on the negative consequences of these behaviours, the issue deserves attention by management. Many social service organisations, however, tend to be characterised by a lack of structure in terms of management and operation. Indeed, many are small organisations with management that possesses minimal knowledge and skills in human resource issues, or none at all (Byrne, 1990; Devlin and Struthers, 1995; Industry Commission, 1994). With the current contraction of the welfare state placing more pressure than ever before on workers and management to be accountable, effective and efficient (Healy, 1997), the experience of employees within these workplaces requires a thorough examination. We need to open our eyes to the possibility that these behaviours occur in social service organisations, in spite of the vital role they play. We need to challenge the stereotypes that can make it difficult to see that 'incongruent' behaviours occur in the helping professions.

References

Barker, R (1995) *The Social Work Dictionary*. Washington, DC: NASW Press.

Bowie, V (1989) *Coping with Violence: A Guide for the Human Services*. Sydney: Karibuni Press.

Brady, E (1993) *Coping with Violent Behaviour: A Handbook for Social Work Staff*. Harlow: Longman.

Braye, S and Preston-Shoot, M (1995) *Empowering Practice in Social Care*. Buckingham: Open University Press.

Brennan, WJ (1996) 'Coping with Aggression and Violence at Work' 14(8) *Safety and Health Practitioner* 46–8.

Brill, N (1995) *Working with People: The Helping Process* (4th edn). New York: Longman.

Byrne, J (1990) *Report on the Community Services Industry: Scope and Definitions*. Canberra: Steering Committee of the Community Services Industry Training and Advisory Committee.

Devlin, M and Struthers, K (1995) *Managing to Make a Difference: A Study of the Management Issues Experienced by Community Service Organisations in Queensland and Strategies to Improve Community Sector Management*. Brisbane: QCOSS.

Einarsen, S (2000a) 'Harassment and Bullying at Work: A Review of the Scandinavian Approach' 5(4) *Aggression and Violent Behaviour* 379–401.

Einarsen, S (2000b) 'Bullying and Harassment at Work: Unveiling an Original Taboo', in M Sheehan, S Ramsay and J Patrick (eds), *Transcending Boundaries: Integrative People, Processes and Systems*. Brisbane: School of Management, Griffith University.

Germain, C and Gitterman, A (1996) *The Life and Model of Social Work Practice: Advances in Theory and Practice* (2nd edn). New York: Columbia University Press.

Harris, R (1997) 'Power', in M Davies (ed), *The Blackwell Companion to Social Work*. Oxford: Blackwell Publishers, pp 28–33.

Hasenfeld, Y (ed) (1992) *Human Services as Complex Organisations*. California: Sage Publications.

Healy, K (1997) 'And for the Activists? A Discussion on the Tensions and Possibilities for Practice Evaluation in Activist Social Work'. Conference Proceedings of the Social Work Influencing Outcomes Conference, Australian Association of Social Workers, Barton, ACT, 21–4 September.

Hoel, H, Rayner, C and Cooper, CL (1999) 'Workplace Bullying' 14 *International Review of Industrial and Organizational Psychology* 195–230.

Industry Commission (1994) 'Charitable Organisations in Australia: An Inquiry into Community Welfare Organisations', Draft Report.

Likert, R (1932) 'A Technique for the Measurement of Attitudes' 140 *Archives of Psychology*.

Maslach, C (1982) *Burnout: The Cost of Caring*. Englewood Cliffs, NJ: Prentice-Hall.

Newhill, C (1996) 'Prevalence and Risk Factors for Client Violence toward Social Workers' 77 *Families in Society* (October) 488–95.

O'Connor, I, Wilson, J and Setterlund, D (1998) *Social Work and Welfare Practice.* Melbourne: Longman.

Pines, A, Aronson, E and Kafry, D (1980) *Burnout.* New York: Free Press.

Rey, L (1996) 'What Social Workers Need to Know about Client Violence' 77(1) *Families in Society* 33–9.

Rothman, J (1994) *Case Management and Community-based Service.* Englewood Cliffs, NJ: Prentice-Hall.

Scheafor, B, Horejsi, C and Horejsi, G (1997) *Techniques and Guidelines for Social Work Practice* (4th edn). Boston: Allyn & Bacon.

Taylor, B and Devine, T (1993) *Assessing Needs and Planning Care in Social Work.* Aldershot: Ashgate.

Chapter 4

Systems Bullying (The Police)

Michael Kennedy

The systems bullying profiled in the following discussion emerges at the meeting of several trajectories of power, status and interest, including those of police culture, restructuring and commissions of inquiry into corruption. The profile draws on experiences at a station with which I am familiar. A particular concern is a reversion to public spectacle as a form of punishment in external and internal inquiry procedures. Whilst I am not defending the role of the police in this examination of systems bullying, procedures that are unreasonable, unethical and infringe on employees' rights deserve scrutiny in all facets of a social democracy. Indeed, unreasonable levels of supervision by intrusive audit and surveillance in the police are likely to mirror those in many occupations and professions in the current climate. In discussing this topic, I would add that any individual implying it is possible to rid a competitive and capitalist society of corruption is presenting an uninformed solution to an oxymoron.

The Rise of Policing and Police Culture

The need for organised law enforcement in a liberal democracy is explained by Locke (1690), in that people are better off forfeiting some of their rights to an authority whose coercive power will protect life and property. The nineteenth century saw the birth of the modern police in an industrial era marked by an epidemic of poverty, low wages, poor working and living conditions, and the exploitation of the labour market by the new middle class. In these conditions, unprecedented social unrest justified the state's formation of police as a social control apparatus to protect middle-class commercial and property interests.

The police culture is one of working-class origins. Compared with other professions in the socio–welfare–criminal justice system, police were poorly educated and yet exposed to enormous levels of conflict and corruption. Some suggest that police service was an opportunity for working-class men to become socially mobile. Others argue that police were in the main rejected by their own class and never accepted by the middle class. In either case the police have developed their own history, their own language and their own culture, and arguably, a 'false consciousness' relating to social mobility. And so, from their capitalist origins, the police, by consent or otherwise, have been manipulated and bullied by the state to do the bidding of the bourgeoisie. The desired outcome has been social control, albeit at the cost of oppressing the less privileged.

The action of state agencies is more often than not impartial. Theories of radical criminology suggest that the less privileged are over-represented within criminal justice because the system has been engineered to control working-class and underclass elements constructed as unruly. Preoccupation with these strata is seen to divert public attention from flaws and injustices of the bourgeoisie capitalist system. In this vein, social control, crime and crime control are depicted as bewildering, odious and managed by legislation, law enforcement and stereotyping to sustain an unequal class structure (Rock, 1997).

A comprehensive explanation of the ways in which dynamics such as systems bullying come to be normalised in networks of power and authority has been provided by Foucault (1975; see also Fillingham, 1993). Initially, torture was a crucial part of criminal investigation and the trial was part of the punishment. After the trial, the sovereign power of the state usually required an execution that was a public spectacle, so as to make an example of the perpetrator. However, during the eighteenth-century, society began to question the public spectacle of torture and death of prisoners. Eventually the practice was replaced in democracies by what was perceived as a more civilised, considerate system of solitary punishment and imprisonment.

During this transition, most of the public outrage towards public torture, punishment and the death penalty was directed at the state through the executioner, not through the sentencing judge, court officials or state prosecutor. Foucault suggests that the role of the executioner has since been sanitised to become those of the policeman and prison officer. As the executioner was easily demonised, so now are police and prison officers. Bentham's nineteenth-century prison panopticon and supervision have become a form of discipline, which after a while can create the illusion that every movement and thought is being observed, not only for the observed but also for the observer. In prisons, constant observation and a penalty for the slightest infraction of the rules was, and is still, the beginning of the disciplinary or punishment process. Those prisoners nged into docile workers by the dynamics of discipline and surveil- ... mply return to prison as recidivists, as Foucault explains (1975).

Understanding of the panopticon's operation enables us to see the ways in which surveillance and discipline are enacted through modern technology. Drivers' licences, health care, criminal records, pensions, public housing, local government rates, mailing lists, newspapers, television and radio can all be seen as exercises in surveillance. All contribute to the construction of the citizen a compliant commodity and the surveillant/ police as a more compliant servant of the state.

Although the issue of police corruption had been raised earlier on occasions, there was generally little scrutiny of the Australian police as an institution until the 1970s. About this time a number of international issues, such as the Vietnam War and apartheid in South Africa, had created social unrest and public demonstrations. At the same time a world recession related to rising oil prices placed the Australian welfare state under pressure, and unemployment rose to unprecedented levels, particularly amongst the unskilled and working class. Also, opiate and other substance abuse created a need for cash, which was not available through legitimate means for the majority of individuals reliant on drugs. Added to this, almost the entire Western world adopted economic rationalism as a management tool. This trend was reflected in the move to quantitative measures of productivity as a basis for assessing the merit of the police organisation and individual police officers within it. These measures were accompanied by an aggressive and competitive promotion system in many law enforcement organisations. In many instances the increase or decrease in crime and the road toll was statistically aligned to arrest rates or infringement notices, and so productivity was, and arguably still is, measured in arrest rates and fines.

The subconscious and often conscious justification police use for being heavy handed, even to the point of being brutal, is often that the ends justify the means. An explanation of this logic may be derived from Durkheim's theory of *anomie* (Bilton et al, 1996). As anomie, crime and social unrest are a form of social ill-health that manifests itself as a result of strains arising from the breakdown of a society's norms and values. In turn, this breakdown is seen as a consequence of unrestricted desires and a modern competitive society. In crude terms, we are all born bad and we need rules to survive. In these terms, a conservative state often encourages police to see themselves as the thin blue line separating good from bad.

All of this is happening in a society that is moving from collective to individual thinking in a very competitive and ruthless atmosphere. In these conditions, many police see themselves as propping up a weak system in order to keep society safe. In the past an average police officer was not prepared academically, emotionally or politically to deal with either a nonconformist and radical society or a progressive and tolerant criminal justice system. Here I can speak from personal experience as a police officer.

Police, Professionals, and Reformers

At regular joint agency meetings with the Department of Public Prosecutions, the Health Department, and Family and Community Services, the average police officer, including myself, struggled to understand the language and politics of the various ideologies that were driving the criminal justice–health–welfare debate. Whilst there is some conflict between the human service disciplines, psychology and sociology are generally united in criticism of the criminal justice system. What all of these professions had in common, as distinct from understandings of the police and corrective services, can be explained as '*Verstehen*'. In Max Weber's terms, *Verstehen* signifies knowledge and understanding as to how people in a capitalist society decide which direction in life they will follow and what status they will achieve (Bilton et al, 1996).

The intellectual exclusion of most police, even educated police, by human service–legal professionals in most policy discussion is a similar division that is still maintained. Indeed, I have learnt through my own university studies that this form of exclusion bullying is fostered and promoted at almost all levels in academic and policy communities. The reasons as to why the proletariat is over-represented in the criminal justice system and why the police are often excluded in the criminal justice–health–welfare debate are arguably the same. Of concern, these constructions of criminality and policing tends to divert attention to the base of criminal justice status and the class pyramid, and away from a flawed patriarchal and class-driven criminal justice system and its privileged professional patrons.

In Australia, affirmative action recruitment policies of the 1980s were, without doubt, a breath of fresh air for most police organisations. They attracted a diverse range of individuals who previously would never have considered the police as a career. Along with the new recruiting strategy came an emphasis on higher education, and a small but significant number of police took advantage of a generous public service study policy in order to be more competitive in the promotion stakes. Unfortunately, the knowledge obtained by educated police in many instances was not shared with colleagues or used to benefit the organisation collectively. A competitive and individualistic culture became very much a part of the police service. Uneducated and often unambitious police with hands-on experience were pushed to one side by many of the new educated elite. This elite tended to pursue personal achievement and to declare that the 'dinosaurs' had very little to contribute to the new order of things.

It was often distressing to see good and earnest police struggling to understand why their opinions held no currency or value. However, the dominant discourse on most criminal justice–health–welfare reform took place and still takes place in a very corporatist atmosphere, which seldom includes those who provide the direct public service.

Several forces shape the requirements of officers in the reformed police service. Individual officers are somehow expected to work within ideologies of the humanities professions, which are principally rooted in humanistic approaches to social welfare. They must also negotiate a predominantly liberal and adversarial legal system that emphasises winners and losers. Their performance must also meet competitive, economic rationalist ideals of a political system that is notably conservative and market-driven. Striving to engage with this level of professional diversity has the potential to produce outcomes that incite a broad range of criticisms. The diversity and the sometimes contradictory nature of these demands certainly makes the analysis and critique of law enforcement easier, albeit from an antagonistic and lofty perch.

Figure 4.1 (see p 39), from Barr (1995: 123), represents a field of tensions in the relations of power between key players engaged in the defining of needs and determining of responses in the system. Barr's schema alerts us to the potential for disempowerment in the system. While this model of power distribution is simplistic, as Barr acknowledges, what it does explain is that there has to be mutual agreement between the state/professionals and the community in order that power is not so unevenly distributed through the complex web of relations as to disempower either group. The same principle could apply within the state and to its professionals, including the various agencies making up the criminal justice–health–welfare system or management and staff of the various bureaucracies. The power web involving organisations, professions and individuals requires a healthy balance of empowerment to be functional, whereas its dysfunctioning is often due to significant disempowerment of particular groups.

Scapegoating the Police

Modern political parties commonly display intense commitment to staying in power, whatever the cost. Allowing agencies of the state to be

Figure 4.1 Definition of needs

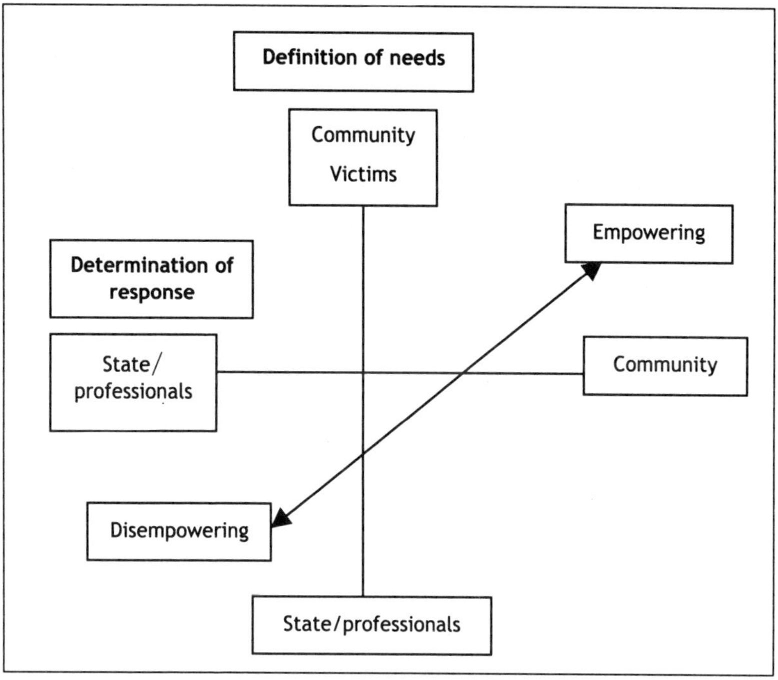

marginalised and scapegoated to these ends seems no longer such a political disadvantage. Indeed, welfare workers, police, teachers and health care professionals, armed services and corrective service personnel have all been sacrificed for political expediency, at one time or another, in recent years.

The New South Wales Wood Royal Commission into police corruption was a very foregone conclusion by the time it took place in the mid-1990s. Not surprisingly, the majority of corruption exposed by examination in public was from the various drug investigation areas. Also, a number of corrupt State and federal police identified in the Commission had been mentioned in earlier corruption investigations and inquiries. A factor that abets such investigations of police is that, although police have enormous levels of power in dealing with the public, they have little power and status within their own organisations to protect themselves. A disadvantage is that corruption inquiries generally only affect or sway police who have a conscience, whilst those without a conscience can often survive any level of scrutiny. There is conflicting debate about the threshold of the success of corruption inquiries in a competitive society where market morality is the norm, and money and material possessions the commodities shaping values.

Police Culture, Stress and Reform

The existence of a police culture, of police corruption, and of the continual exposure of operational police to trauma, conflict, violence and high levels of stress, are a fact of life. In this context, a problem for the outsider is the unconditional cultural solidarity encountered when one attempts to negotiate the various nodes and capillaries of the criminal justice power web. Often this web includes some corruption at every intersection.

Herman's (1992) study of stress among military personnel provides useful insights into experiences in the police. Poor supervision and ineffective management of stress in the military are identified as factors that can amplify what is otherwise a very manageable disorder, to the point of creating post-traumatic stress symptoms. Herman reminds us of a time these symptoms were dealt with more brutally. For example, soldiers suffering from shell shock or battle fatigue in the First World War were bullied, humiliated, even shot, in order that their comrades would soldier on and behave like men. In later years, treatment strategies altered and were designed to minimise the separation between a soldier and his comrades. Informal debriefings among colleagues and a strong degree of camaraderie and leadership often were the strongest protection against stress associated with terror and dread. However, the dilemma is that the cultural-social glue bonding those in stressful professions, whilst necessary for competent functioning, is the same cultural glue that enables entrenched corruption to survive.

Some would say the typical police personality includes authoritarianism, suspicion, bullying, hostility, insecurity, conservatism and cynicism. However, those who promote this perspective are hard pressed to present any responsive evidence to support this view. Evidence may be provided by way of personal experience, but most seems to be anecdotal. This is not to say that many police do not at one time or other hold prejudices. Indeed, evidence presented by Hollin (1989: 126–51) supports the inference that police personality and values are socialised by prevailing values or *Verstehen* in police culture. This evidence is derived from an examination of a broad range of psychometric studies including those by Clucas, Potter, Gudjonsson and Adlam, Hunt, Reiner, and Hochstedler (cited in Hollin, 1989). In the light of this evidence, it could be concluded that renovating the shape of police culture is a better social alternative to demolishing and rebuilding the culture.

Power, Corruption and Reform by Destruction

A comprehensive insight into the micro-politics of power in the web of relations in policing may be derived from Foucault's investigation of the relations of power and knowledge (see Smart, 1985). From Foucault we learn that dominance is related more to the relations of power and knowledge enfolded in a discourse, or ways of seeing and acting, than to truth values. Also, in the exercise of power, positions are taken and identities formed as a positive strategic accommodation to the problems of everyday life. In the web of power and knowledge relations in the police, then, corruption is only one dynamic, and may thus be variously concentrated or diffused throughout. Some nodes may be corrupt, others not, but all are interconnected through policies, systems, procedures, and individual and group action.

Application of Foucault's scenario to the police raises questions as to the feasibility of minimising or attempting to eliminate corruption by destroying the police power web. We are brought to the realisation that destruction of the power web may be misplaced, since much of the power exercised in the web is positive, well intentioned and unrelated to corruption, notwithstanding that it may be sometimes misused.

Foucault's mapping of the transition from brutal and uncivilised practices of sovereign authority to more sanitised expressions of punishment in contemporary democracies, also raises questions as to the function of public spectacles and humiliation in public inquiries. Indeed, the presenting of video and tape-recorded surveillance of suspects through the media by tribunals and commissions of inquiry appears as a regression to an earlier, more brutal form of punishment. Of concern, the use of public spectacle and humiliation in the New South Wales corruption inquiry reproduced a more arrogant and uncivilised expression of sovereign justice. The public spectacle of punishment and humiliation, long abandoned by Western democracies on the basis that it was unjust, appeared to have returned.

Conclusion

In attempting to destroy the police power web, the Royal Commission and subsequently the Police Integrity Commission appear to have embraced inquisitorial investigative styles. Most of the public has been duped into thinking these tribunals and commissions have the authority of the state to determine guilt or innocence and impose a punishment. However, this is not the case, since these inquiries only gather evidence, which should then be presented at proper criminal courts for verdicts to be justly determined and sentences to be imposed in an impartial and civil manner.

In recent years, these special tribunals and commissions seem to have acted as de facto processes for determining guilt and imposing sentence through using the media for the public spectacle of punishment and humiliation. As such they could be considered to have abused democratic processes and civil rights. Concerns as to this modus operandi are reflected in the rise of suicides of people of interest (not all related to allegations of criminal behaviour) to double figures during the New South Wales Royal Commission. These outcomes were seen by many as a form of execution by public spectacle. At the very least, one could reasonably regard these processes as a form of *systems bullying.*

Arguably, these processes contribute to the dismantling of the camaraderie necessary to enable law enforcement both to function and to manage its stresses. Beyond the police, the public has just cause for concern as to behaviours of a state engaged in management of members of its own statutory bodies by public spectacle and humiliation. A state that condones such practices could well inflict similar procedures on the broader community. Rather than destroying the web of relations that constitutes policing, cultural change could proceed more effectively as part of an overall involvement, from top to bottom and laterally and collectively. Such a program could involve all the nodes and capillaries of the power web, as they intervene in people's lives on behalf of the state.

The process of cultural change could well avoid a positivist ideology of more law and more order, as this is often executed without justice or humanity. This contradiction is examined in Hugo's (1970) novel, *Les misérables.* Therein, the positivist Javert pursues the petty criminal Jean Valjean because *the law is the law.* In the end the ideological obsession of Javert renders Jean Valjean a victim, partly because of the injustice of the law, but mostly because of Javert's single-minded obsession.

For the results of a cultural change program to have a positive, trickle-down effect in the community, the policy of large corporations and the state (in the case of police) of intervention in internal affairs would be more effective with a kinder, softer and more forgiving touch. This is particularly so in the present climate, where discretion withdrawn from professionals who are service providers is discretion withdrawn from the public. And accountability heaped onto a professional in any bureaucracy is accountability heaped onto the community. We should be warned that service providers who are disempowered and treated as commodities have a tendency to treat the service users in the same way.

Police, in turn, have to accept that if they are granted powers, there is a price relating to police accountability and the level of scrutiny that can be imposed on the gatekeeper by their own bureaucracy and the state. When concepts and policies fail across capitalist society, winners and losers have to be determined in order that blame can be apportioned. One thing is for sure – blame seldom fastens itself onto the self-anointed or privileged few who develop such policies, and spokespersons of the contemporary state, globally, have a tendency to holler the legal defence of '*liability*' to justify their silence.

References

Barr, A (1995) 'Empowering Communities Beyond Fashionable Rhetoric' 30(2) *Community Development Journal* 121–32.

Bilton, T, Bonnett, K, Jones, P, Skinner, D, Stanworth, M and Webster, A (1996) *Introductory Sociology*. London: Macmillan.

Foucault, M (1975) *Surveiller et punir* [Discipline and Punish]. Paris: Editions Gallimard.

Fillingham, L (1993) *Foucault for Beginners*. London: Writers & Readers.

Herman, J (1992) *Trauma and Recovery*. London: Basic Books.

Hugo, V (1970) *Les misérables*. Paris: Romans Complètes (originally published 1862).

Hollin, C (1989) *Psychology and Crime*. London: Routledge.

Locke, J (1690) 'Second Trieste of Civil Government', in J Kleinig (ed) (1987), *Ways of Understanding the Police Role*. New York: John Jay College of Criminal Justice.

Rock, P (1997) 'Sociological Theories of Crime', in M Maguire, R Morgan and R Reiner (eds), *The Oxford Handbook of Criminology*. Oxford: Clarendon Press.

Smart, B (1985) *Michel Foucault*. London: Routledge Press.

Chapter 5

Cultures of Secrecy, Abuse and Bullying

Paradoxes in Religious Organisations, Families and Social Networks

Cara Beed

Introduction

Organisations where secrecy, abuse and bullying behaviour dominate relationships are typified by certain cultures. In this chapter I suggest ways to monitor organisational structures and processes, and it is important that these structures and processes be examined. Individuals who express their personal autonomy authoritatively tend to be better equipped to challenge secretive, abusive and bullying cultures. Secrecy, abuse and bullying are difficult and fraught areas of human relationships and social organisations.

Accountability and public awareness through education are needed. A culture of awareness reduces the potential for abuse, and independent intervention and appropriate legislation can further address secrecy, abuse and bullying in all organisations. Thirty-five specific suggestions (Beed, 1999; 2000) are listed to assist the individual in developing an awareness of abusive, secretive and bullying cultures in personal relationships, workplaces, social services, community life and government.

Throughout this chapter, structures and processes conducive to spiritual abuse (such as the manipulation of beliefs in cults), emotional abuse and physical abuse are highlighted, particularly those relevant to religious, educational and pastoral care organisations, as groups and individuals offering pastoral relationships are all too easily corrupted. If individuals were educated about these topics, and requested accountability from religious organisations, schools, care organisations and other bodies, change could sweep through the major institutions in society. Social awareness can encourage individuals to develop and maintain the accountable relationships necessary in every arena in society.

Definitions

The following introductory summaries are taken from a more detailed discussion in Beed (1998).

Power

Power is the ability to produce results desired by a particular person or group. Everyone needs power, but when one person imposes his or her power on another, abuse can occur. To exercise power a person needs:

- commitment to an idea;
- a framework in which to work;
- knowledge of how to proceed;
- skills to proceed;
- co-operation from others;
- opportunities to influence others; and,
- opportunities to involve powerful others.

Abuse and bullying

Abuse is anything that hurts another person (Ormerod and Ormerod, 1995: xi), and may be physical, sexual or psychological. Bullying is repeatedly and deliberately placing a person under stress (McCarthy et al, 1996: vii). Bullying and abuse will affect a person's nervous system, and long-term stress can result from this (Wilkie, 1995: 8; McCarthy et al, 1996: vii).

The culture of abuse

The culture of abuse is all the conventions, practices and language used anywhere to hurt, mistreat, malign or revile people. It is all the ways used to injure and maltreat people in all walks of life. Even meetings may be an abusive structure, as can gossip. Typically, whilst highly structured, authoritarian hierarchies allow those at the top of the structure to abuse others, and those in the lowest rank may also adopt abusive behaviours.

The culture of secrecy

The culture of secrecy is the use of dominant social forces to deny truth. Those wanting secrecy use ideas, laws, norms, customs, language, myths, beliefs and institutional rules to prevent the truth being seen or heard.

Powerful forces in society, especially leaders of institutions, may limit disclosure of information about abuse. However, the culture of secrecy should not be confused with privacy or confidentiality. Everyone has the right to privacy, as long as they respect others' rights. Confidentiality is a sound part of therapy, for example, but only while it benefits the client, otherwise it may stop individuals from obtaining help. When confidentiality prevents a person from seeking help, it is 'secrecy', and that is a further form of abuse. Secrecy and silence breed abuse, particularly by isolating an individual from those who can help. In professional services, such as medicine and pastoral care, the culture of secrecy amounts to organised abuse of clients who may already have experienced abuse.

The effect on the community

Bullying, abuse and the culture of secrecy have a harmful effect on the community. Research findings indicating negative impacts of bullying at work that carry over into families, and result in medical care and social security being sought, have been reported (McCarthy et al, 1995). Randall (1997) and Byrne (1994) have also documented degrading effects of neighbourhood bullying, in and between families, in youth settings and in sports clubs. It is important that discussions on abuse recognise that there is also a detailed body of literature on abuse in church-related pastoral care (for example, Beed, 1998; Foley, 1996; Kohl and Crowley, 1998; Last et al, 1994; Ormerod and Ormerod, 1995).

Personal autonomy

Personal autonomy is the right, ability and opportunity for an individual to investigate, adopt and put into practice their own principles and rules of life, with the confidence to co-operate in patterns of interdependence with others. All individuals need these rights and opportunities, which must be independent of coercion, interference or control by others. To be free of abuse, an individual needs some level of personal autonomy (Beed, 1998: 14–18).

Authoritative versus authoritarian relationships

Authoritative relationships have sound verbal 'give-and-take' between all participants, and in these relationships everyone understands why decisions have been made. Policies and actions are fully and openly discussed in order that everyone understand how these policies and actions relate to them and what is being done.

In authoritative relationships people may object to particular policies and actions, and seek to have their own ideas on these discussed. If one person does not agree with a particular decision, it is important that they express their views and their opinions be fully addressed (Baumrind, 1978: 244). Authoritative relationships require both time and sensitive communication. The development of agreed boundaries must be based on individual needs and co-operation (Ochiltree, 1990: 24).

All this is in contrast to authoritarian relationships, which are controlling. Powerful people use their authority to bind other people through the domination of their will. Although authoritarian people may think they are working in the best interests of others, in actuality they are corrupting others' rights.

The contrast lies in the benefits, for example, in an authoritative family grouping, where the social competence of its members is developed. Members embrace their personal autonomy, whilst leading interdependent and co-operative lives. Other benefits include responsible decision-making and actions. Developing interdependent behaviour involves challenges, including engaging in complex discussions that require all members using their social competence with care.

Overcoming Bullying Behaviours

Bullying is the repeated and deliberate abuse of another person, often in secret. It seldom happens where people can exert power in their lives, express their opinions and contribute to what is going on. Where power is shared, it is hard for an individual to use bullying behaviours to gain power over others. However, within an authoritarian group or organisation, this will occur more easily. Where power is exerted from top to bottom, little flexibility exists for individuals to express their own ideas and make contributions. Structures, processes and behaviours in authoritarian groups are controlling and rigid.

Everyone needs some power, and if the structures and processes allow bullying, any one individual has the potential to abuse their power. The gentlest person has the capacity to bully if pushed into an organisational straightjacket of authoritarian edicts and machinations. Only through awareness can bullying behaviours be prevented and co-operative behaviour encouraged to achieve agreed tasks. Focusing on co-operation is a challenge. However, individuals and organisations can be free of bullying through developing an awareness of poor structures and eliminating these from social relationships.

Authoritative cultures

To stop bullying, the structures and processes that encourage this behaviour must be changed. Nurturing social relationships and organisations eople co-operate with others and contributing to activities shared power is an alternative structure that focuses on authoritative relationships.

In authoritative relationships, each person has a developed understanding of what, and why, things are asked of them, agreed to and carried out. Sound give-and-take between all people establishes discussions as vibrant and contributory. Unlike authoritarian structures, where orders are handed down from dominant leaders who do not listen to subordinates, in authoritative relationships everyone seeks to understand others, and aims for a co-operative framework.

Building authoritative relationships and interdependent behaviour involves many challenges, particularly through engaging in highly developed discussions between all those involved. Authoritative people share power and use their personalities to contribute to the community for themselves and others. They do not exercise power regardless of others' needs. In authoritative relationships, secrecy, abuse and bullying become rare.

Authoritative relationships involve the need to express personal power, and to recognise and practise expressing personal autonomy. The positive outcomes are shared resolutions of dilemmas in social relationships. Each person develops a comprehensive sense of self and an expression of her or his personal autonomy in all situations. Authoritative expression of this personal autonomy can only be achieved through appropriate structures and processes in the home, the workplace, school, sports activities, social clubs and social networks. These networks need to be the type that encourages each individual to be positive about who and what they are.

Authoritative relationships versus authoritarian structures

Bullying involves a culture of abuse, in which its conventions, practices and language can be used within a group or an organisation to mistreat, malign and revile members. It can even extend to people outside an organisation. It is the sum total of the ways of acting that can be used to injure and maltreat both people involved in an organisation and those outside it. Even mismanaging a community meeting can allow bullying and lead to abuse.

Typically, the culture of abuse is practised in hierarchical mode, extending from those in superior control in an organisation to those in subordinate positions, and through all ranks of the organisation. Another aspect of bullying, where the culture of secrecy is very dominant, is secrecy about abusive behaviour. Individuals who bully often keep the extremes of their behaviour secret, ensuring their victims hide the abuse due to fear, and isolating the victims from peer and other support.

Power exerted over others is corruptive, whilst power developed in co-operation with others produces a pooling of strengths, directed to the common good.

Personal autonomy and authoritative action

To be free of bullying, or abuse, some level of personal autonomy is required. Our sense of self is socialised from our earliest days. We are socialised to comply with the society around us, to inhibit our natural desires, and to contain our demands, so adjusting to those around us. This works well for the overall organisation of society, especially where there is a balance in demands for time and attention. An awareness and appreciation of essential human needs is vital, and should be encouraged. The outcome is knowledge of who we are within the social environment. Too often, the social milieu in which we live dictates behaviours and false needs that alienate our self-awareness, until ultimately, we fail to recognise our true needs. Indeed, some individuals have little sense of self, no personal autonomy and thereby become vulnerable to control by others. Co-operating with the social networks of a family grouping, workplace, school, religious organisation and community need not extend to denying self-awarcness or needs, or the acceptance of bullying, the sacrifice of personal opinions or acting against one's will. Co-operating in the community is one thing; unquestioning acceptance of bullying, and the structures that encourage it, is quite another.

New Social Relationships for a New Millennium

The distinguishing of right and wrong is a major task for all peoples. In world conflicts, opposing groups defend differing views of right and wrong, with the means to achieving peace and charity in the world at large appearing difficult to attain, and bullying behaviour predominates in forceful displays of armed aggression.

Unfortunately, socialisation can train individuals to suppress their autonomy to such a degree that they conform to authoritarian hierarchical structures, which are ultimately destructive. Frequently, the activities of an individual who bullies leads to an acceptance of this behaviour, which then continues. The genocide in East Timor is just one example of extreme bullying behaviour, tolerated elsewhere in the world for 24 years.

Where authoritative people express their values and insist on being heard, change occurs. Where schools, workplaces, political parties and service groups have reduced top-heavy authoritarian structures, conformity and obedience in the less powerful is weakened. Some groups decide on shared goals and agree achievement parameters, and co-operative patterns develop.

Authoritative relationships

But what of personal relationships, religious organisations, government or educational institutions where co-operation and authoritative relationships are not recognised as vital? Where authoritarianism still dominates relationships, the community suffers from the outcomes. This is particularly so in the case of workplace bullying, and also in education where differing goals cause dissension in the home, school and wider community. It is in authoritarian structures where bullying behaviours encroach on the independence, work satisfaction and health of many individuals. The degrees of achievement of the overall community at all levels are also inhibited.

It is true that authoritarian behaviour is not as common as it was in the eighteenth century or even in the early nineteenth century. Nonetheless, in the new millennium, authoritarian organisations continue to dominate and bullying behaviour to thrive in them. We need to guard against the distinctive patterns in authoritarian structures and processes that encourage bullying behaviours. The benefits of authoritative relationships, in personal relationships, the workplace, schools, religious organisations and the community, enhance social competence and lift society to new levels of social interaction. All people in authoritative relationships can embrace their personal autonomy and lead interdependent and co-operative lives.

Knowledge of what is happening in organisations will aid a clearer understanding of the behaviours occurring and will challenge any abusive and bullying behaviours. The following 35 suggestions provide a beginning for the examination of organisations in which individuals and their family members are active.

Monitoring Cultures of Secrecy, Abuse and Bullying

(1) Monitor the structures of the organisations in which you or your family participate.

(2) Monitor activities for the presence of abuse, secrecy, isolation and exhaustion.

(3) Monitor whether you or your family members can achieve your life goals.

(4) Monitor groups for conformity to inflexible rules and hierarchical rituals.

(5) List the demanded, but unwritten, codes of behaviour that feature in the activities.
(6) Monitor whether 'failure' is a judgment made about individuals or the group.
(7) Who takes the credit for 'success'? Are 'favourites' often seen as successful?
(8) How are rewards and praise distributed, and by whom?
(9) Is the leader the focus of all activities, and who is the leader?
(10) Monitor any time, or patterns of time, spent in isolation with a powerful person.
(11) Monitor for ethical responses, to all activities, structures and issues in the group.
(12) Expect and demand private and public behaviours that are open, accountable and ethical.
(13) Monitor the health of members of your family for 'stress'.
(14) Check all details of committees, finances, accountability, leaders and staff qualifications.
(15) Monitor leaders' and participants' behaviours for signs of misuse of power.
(16) Become part of the culture of awareness about misuses of power and subsequent difficulties in the community.
(17) List the social aspects involved in the organisation's program.
(18) Emphasise, develop and appreciate the concept of personal autonomy.
(19) Be aware of commitments your family members make to individuals or groups.
(20) Monitor the role-modelling provided by the adults and other leaders in the group.
(21) Monitor the role-modelling of the adults and leaders in the group for their use of power.
(22) Appreciate and demand acknowledgment of filial links and sound family structures.
(23) Emphasise the connection of family life to the wider community.
(24) Be educated about individuals becoming excessively committed to authoritarian groups.
(25) Expect and insist that organisations respect the family unit.
(26) Monitor whether problems or difficulties are acknowledged in the organisation, or whether only a constant image of success portrayed.
(27) Does anyone in your organisation pirate or plagiarise your ideas or work, presenting these as their own without acknowledgment or recognition of the source?

(28) Does your organisation promote donations of money, property or valuables in ways that embarrass you into giving beyond your means, or beyond the levels of giving in other contemporaneous groups?

(29) Question organisations where gossip is shared, especially where gossip-sharing emphasises one person's importance whilst others are diminished.

(30) Investigate whenever you ever feel uncomfortable about any aspect of the organisation, individuals, activities or controls, such as secrecy.

(31) Be wary if leaders of any organisation prevaricate rather than address your questions or requests for action.

(32) The only conceivable excuse for secrecy is a joyous outcome, such as an acceptable surprise birthday party or an acceptable surprise present at birthdays or Christmas.

(33) Is there any fear or threat in any activity, conversation, idea or belief?

(34) Do activities or resolutions of problems revolve around isolation and removal from personal relationships, the wider society and educational parameters?

(35) Does a leader bridle at the idea of a second opinion on the course of action to be taken by the group member or their family?[1]

Conclusion

When people can authoritatively resolve the dilemmas in their social relationships and organisations, resolutions are positive. It is vital for every person to have an effective sense of self to express personal autonomy in all situations. This authoritative expression of personal autonomy can only be achieved through the structures and processes in all areas of society being the type to encourage each individual to be happy with, and expressive of, who and what they are. This is particularly so for children as they mature through school and social activities. It is also important for any minority group attempting to lead authoritative lives in an authoritarian society. The material presented above comprises suggestions for everybody, especially families, for examining the structures and processes of any organisations with which they are involved. It is equally applicable to the workplace, indeed, to any organisation in society. We need to monitor the relationships, structures and processes in the organisations, groups and networks we are members of, and if we develop authoritative relationships, with no characteristics of authoritarianism, we can expect major changes throughout human society.

Note

With the publisher's permission, this material is drawn from the author's three earlier publications (Beed, 1998; 1999; 2000). The available literature and observations in the arena inspired interest in these issues, but mindful of legal parameters, no person or group is identified. Unless otherwise stated explicitly, nothing within my publications should be interpreted to refer to myself, my family, or anyone else with whom we have associated.

1 For further details of the 35 suggestions, see Beed (1999; 2000).

References

Baumrind, D (1978) 'Parental Disciplinary Patterns and Social Competence in Children' 9(3) *Youth and Society* 239–76.

Beed, C (1998) *Cultures of Secrecy and Abuse: A Paradox for Churches.* Melbourne: Published by the author.

Beed, C (1999) *Families Can Monitor for Cultures of Secrecy, Abuse and Bullying.* Melbourne: Published by the author.

Beed, C (2000) *Be Attentive: Stop Secrecy, Abuse and Bullying.* Melbourne: Published by the author.

Byrne, B (1994) *Bullying: A Community Approach.* Dublin: Columba Press.

Foley, S (1996) 'Who Hears? Who Listens? Who Pretends?' Conference proceedings of the Inaugural Australian and New Zealand Conference: Sexual Exploitation by Health Professionals, Psychotherapists and Clergy, Committee against Health Professionals and Clergy Abuse, Sydney, 12–14 April.

Kohl, T and Crowley, M (1998) *Not the Way of Christ: The Report of the Independent Pastoral Inquiry into Sexual Misconduct by Clergy or Officers of the Anglican Diocese of Tasmania with Particular Reference to Paedophilia.* Hobart: Anglican Diocese of Tasmania.

Last, H, Gonzalez, M and Vadasz, D (eds) (1994) *Public Pain, Private Pain: Anglican Report about Violence against Women and Abuse of Power within the Church Community.* Melbourne: Centre Against Sexual Assault, Royal Women's Hospital.

McCarthy, P, Sheehan, M and Kearns, D (1995) *Managerial Styles and Their Effects on Employees' Health and Well-Being in Organisations Undergoing Restructuring.* Brisbane: School of Organisational Behaviour and Human Resource Management, Griffith University.

McCarthy, P, Sheehan, M and Wilkie, W (eds) (1996) *Bullying: Causes, Costs and Cures.* Brisbane: Beyond Bullying Association.

Ochiltree, G (1990) *Children in Australian Families.* Melbourne: Longman Cheshire.

Ormerod, N and Ormerod, T (1995) *When Ministers Sin: Sexual Abuse in the Churches.* Sydney: Millennium.

Randall, P (1997) *Adult Bullying: Perpetrators and Victims.* London: Routledge.

Wilkie, W (1995) *Understanding Stress Breakdown* (3rd edition). Sydney: Millennium Books.

Chapter 6

Bullying Using Organisational Procedures

Greg McMahon

Introduction

Perhaps the greatest difference between bullies in the schoolyard and bullies in the boardroom is the scope for boardroom bullies to demean other people using organisational procedures. In the 'schoolyard', most of a bully's power is drawn from a personal physical power over, or personal information about, the bullied person. In the 'boardroom', and in the organisational corridors and lifts leading from them, the bully can exercise positional power. This is an attribute afforded to the bully by the mixture of hierarchies and procedures in an organisation that allow scope for demeaning subordinates and clients through the maladministration of those procedures and through the abuse of those powers.

A description of the bullying that occurs in organisations through the medium of an organisation's procedures for the conduct of its work and its administration is given in the following chapter. The many anecdotes, cases and complaints that have come to the knowledge of the author in duties as a manager, workplace representative, auditor, investigating officer and executive member of a professional association, trade union and two whistleblower organisations are used to give a categorisation of bullying behaviour.

The Individual Bully

To illustrate the bully continuum, 'from schoolyard to boardroom', the following categorisation of procedural bullying in organisations is outlined, using descriptions from the school environment:

- gatekeeper bullying
- sandpit bullying,
- toilet bullying, and
- king bullying.

The gatekeeper bully at school takes up a strategic position, say, on the stairs, at the door to the library, on the walkway across the creek, or the like, and decides who can pass.

In an organisation, gatekeeper bullies deny their subordinates (without reasonable grounds) access to applications, priority over other staff, funds, meetings or briefings necessary to the subordinate's work and training, the experience necessary for gaining qualifications, and the flexibility necessary for family life. Thus, a subordinate may be consistently denied:

- recreation leave during school holidays;
- computer capacity sufficient for standard work software;
- nomination for training that is a prerequisite for promotion;
- attendance at meetings related to their work

Gatekeeper bullies establish barriers to be overcome and gauntlets to be run by colleagues in their working lives.

An organisation heavily influenced or dominated by gatekeeper bullying is relatively slow in the tempo of its operations. Indications of gatekeeper bullying can be a lack of delegation to managers, a lack of initiative among employees, managers limited to working within boundaries, poor communication, little networking amongst staff and poor morale. A relatively large number of personal grievances are lodged within organisations dominated by a gatekeeper bullying culture.

At kindergarten, the gatekeeper bully kept other children from entering or leaving the sandpit. The sandpit bully, on the other hand, kept knocking down or otherwise ruining sandcastles or other structures made by children in the sandpit. This open behaviour included forms where the bully would help build the structure only to destroy it before it could be used or admired. More secretive behavioural forms also occurred. Sandpit bullies stole pieces of the jigsaw puzzle others were putting together, threw the cricket ball into the creek, or ruined the display with graffiti.

In the organisation, sandpit bullies are more proactive than gatekeepers. Sandpit bullies restructure successful teams in order to split them up, assign experts to generalist duties, send achievers on wild goose chases, reassign leaders to tasks without purpose, and take over projects when success is assured. Sandpit bullies also cancel approval for holiday leave without substantial cause, prevent use of company resources for inhouse training, refuse relief arrangements while the bullied are away from the office, and give staff members directions that are ruinous to the relations those individuals have with other staff.

Sandpit bullies are spoilers. Sandpit bullies undermine the progress, achievements, growth and success of targeted individuals in their employ. The situation where the spoiling outcome is greatest for the bully is where the pre-existing condition is excellence or potential excellence. Indicators that an organisation may be heavily influenced or dominated by sandpit bullying is the presence of mediocrity. Mediocrity can be present at both the general level of organisational performance (client satisfaction, productivity) and also at the specific level of individual achievement (qualifications, publications, commendations, outcomes for clients). Achievers leave organisations dominated by sandpit bullying.

At school, the most hurtful bullying was largely associated with the toilet areas and change sheds. These areas were where the school organisation afforded the bully the greatest degree of privacy and freedom from supervision and inspection. These most hurtful forms of bullying include head flushing, slanderous graffiti, physical torture, extortion, removal of clothing, assault, personal ridicule and open threats.

The toilet bully in organisations also prefers to operate where inspection by others is most difficult. The privacy of toilet areas and store rooms is not discarded, but with respect to organisational procedures, the 'privacy' opportunities used by the toilet bully include the one-to-one interview, the counselling interview, the selection interview and the like. The area of greatest operation of the toilet tactics, however, is within the 'privacy' of the *discretionary power* afforded to the superior officer by the organisation in decision-making affecting the subordinate officer.

Instances of toilet bullying, as part of the procedures of an organisation, include falsification and vilification in performance reports, punitive transfers and secondments, personal threats, ridicule and slander during interviews or in 'confidential', 'private', or 'off-the-record' meetings, unjustified referrals for psychological assessment, unfair and unsafe work assignments, hardship rostering patterns, extortion of favours, or coercion into co-operative bullying of others or into complicity with breaches of proper procedures.

Toilet bullies are vengeful. Their aim is to leave a permanent and hurtful mark on the person rather than for that person to experience a temporary frustration in their work. One indicator that an organisation may be heavily influenced or dominated by toilet bullies is a proportionately large number of personal grievances and complaints about supervisors and managers made to external authorities rather than to the organisation itself. There are also likely to be complaints from past bullied employees that they were 'pursued' by the toilet bully in employment, business or professional respects after the bullied employee left the organisation. Repeated performance failures are symptomatic of a toilet-bully culture in an organisation.

The most developed form of the organisational bully is the king bully. At school the king bully had a gang, and they 'expelled' the bullied person from the playground; the bullied person had to either join another gang or leave the school. Territories for gangs were defined, and rules were established, both within gangs and across gangs.

The king bully in an organisation 'expels' workers, expels them from locations, from careers, from favoured groups, from special projects, collaborations or committees, and from organisations. The reason for the expulsion will often appear almost arbitrary, but can typically be for a slight affront; and the expulsion as it is delivered carries with it the strong connotation of 'never to return'. 'It will be as though you never were' is a quote from a movie portrayal of an act of a king bully (*The Charge of the Light Brigade* (1968)).

Within organisations, the king bully is an organisational or locational chief, or professional head, who operates in the open with apparent impunity. Other king bullies are accommodated, their 'territories' even respected. There is no place, however, in the king bully's domain for independents, only favoured officers and hired hands are allowed. Expulsions are effected by subordinate bullies in the organisational 'gang', of the sandpit variety or the toilet variety if the bullied person shows resistance); the 'never-to-return' sentence is enforced by subordinate gatekeeper bullies.

King bully organisations are rogue organisations – they are out of the control of external authorities, such as the shareholders, or the membership, or the government. King bullies are feudal. They are possessed of a sense of 'ownership' of an industry, a sport or other community activity, or of the administration of a public policy. Indications that an organisation is dominated by a king bully are the coexistence, on the one hand, of open and repeated breaches of procedures, with, on the other hand, zero or near-zero grievances by employees. Alienation of the 'clients' of an organisation can develop with organisations ruled by king bullies. King bullies usually have attached to their history one of the classic whistleblower cases from that industry or jurisdiction.

The Organisation as the Bully

The king bully and the rogue organisation are examples of an individual bully and subordinates misusing or abusing the procedures of an organisation in order to exercise their collective need to demean targeted

s. In this situation, the organisation's rules are being misused :d, and the fault lies with the individual, not the organisation.

A pattern of bullying is emerging from case studies, anecdotal evidence, media accounts and law reports. The behaviour of organisations in stress-prevalent situations may be that, at the highest level, some organisations and jurisdictions are legitimising and validating the 'bullying' option as a frontline or fall-back strategy for coping with problems faced by those organisations, industries, or jurisdictions. The facilitation of the bullying option is achieved by a deliberate 'sapping' of the integrity of the organisation's procedures, using the defects that allow the bullying option to be mobilised.

In this case, the value system giving rise to retaining the bullying option is not some residual psychiatric disorder from the schoolyard days of the organisation's chief executive, but is the value system of the boardroom. It is led by that benchmark of values of executive management, namely *pragmatism*. Resorting to the bullying option out of a sense of pragmatism can be a boardroom response to 'impossibilities' in governance experienced or perceived by the boardroom. In the private sector, the perceived impossibilities can be:

- using ethical practices in a competitive marketplace;
- complying with the law whilst meeting commercial expectations of majority shareholders.

The impossibilities can be remarkably similar for their counterparts in the public sector:

- competing on a level playing field with the private sector, whilst held to the accountability burdens of the public sector;
- enforcing laws that are detrimental to the commercial interests of major industries.

The public relations (PR), organisational development (OD), chief legal officer (CLO), human resource management (HRM), equal employment opportunities (EEO) and industrial relations (IR) work units are expected to construct an edifice of compliance with the ethical, legal, accountability, or enforcement imperatives of the organisation. However, in order to ensure workplace compliance with the pragmatic strategies adopted by executive management to cope with these so-called impossibilities, the bullying option may be taken up.

Establishment of the bully option for the organisation requires the same degree of sophistication as is required for setting up the more respectable management control systems adopted by responsible executives to ensure congruence by staff with organisational goals. Aspects of such management control systems (see Figure 6.1, p 59) include:

Figure 6.1 Aspects of management control systems (adapted from 'Framework for evaluation management control systems', in Horngren and Foster, 1987)

- strategic planning,
- industry economics,
- organisational structure,
- managerial style,
- organisational culture.

The parallels in establishing the bully option include the following:

- Strategic planning and scenario development processes, using the results of analyses of the competitive environment faced by the organisation, can be used to demonstrate the 'impossibility' faced by the organisation, and to explain the need for the pragmatic solution. Debate can identify areas of opposition to the pragmatic strategy, and afford examples of how opponents to the pragmatic option will be treated.
- The formal organisation's structure can be subordinated to the purpose of securing control of the implementation of the bully strategy. Restructuring can be used to release non-dependable staff. The procedures for restructuring can provide opportunities where candidates for key positions, including PR, OD, HRM, EEO, CLO and IR, can be given acting appointments in these roles and then made to submit to 'integrity tests' concerning the implementation of the procedures of restructuring. These integrity tests give the acting appointees the opportunity to demonstrate their commitment to the pragmatic solution.

- The managerial style favoured by the need to implement the bully option can become essentially coercive, rewards and punishments being derived according to displays of 'loyalty' or 'disloyalty'. Paternalism can develop, particularly towards those who are 'found out' by external authorities because of breakdowns in the PR/OD/HRM/EEO/CLO/IR edifice.
- The dominant emotion in this organisational culture can become fear, whether that be a fear of being 'found out', or a fear of not complying with the pragmatic stratagem. Executive chiefs can respond to the first fear by exercising displays of bully power so as to reassure the actively compliant, and to give reminders to the passively compliant.

A dynamic to the procedures of organisations implementing the bully option is the role in those procedures of what can be termed 'innocent parties'. Innocent parties are an essential part of the PR/OD/HRM/EEO/CLO/IR edifice behind which the bullying proceeds, for their innocence lends credibility to the façade. An 'innocent party' is a party to the bullying procedure whose contribution to the procedure is without blemish.

However, that contribution is only part of a total procedure that contains the act of bullying. Particularly where the innocent party is at the far end of the process, without the opportunity to question the outcome of the procedures completed prior to their contribution, their innocent contribution can be used to represent the total procedure. Consultants, external investigators, auditors and staff can also find themselves in this 'innocent party' role. Examples of 'innocent party' contributions to overall bullying procedures can include:

- participating in public relations events, videos or brochures that misrepresent or mislead in their presented form;
- completing reviews and investigations, in conformity with prejudicial terms of reference;
- participating on selection panels for positions already compromised by irregularities in the procedures earlier in the selection process (for example, restricted advertisement, bias in the selection criteria);
- provision of an opinion on the legality of a proposed action, to a brief based on information selected to avoid critical legal impediments;
- conduct of disciplinary procedures against an individual, driven or provoked to the breach of procedure by bullying, or denied a proper defence by the destruction of evidence or the intimidation of witnesses.

An indication that an organisation is operating with the bully option may be any display by the watchdogs within an organisation of tolerance for, or covering up of, breaches by the organisation in their respective areas of responsibility. The 'watchdogs' include, for example, the governance board, auditor, safety officer, quality assurance chief, EEO ombudsman, or environmental chief. Where the tolerance and cover up extends to anti-corruption bodies within that jurisdiction, to its grievance bureaux, its public prosecutors, ombudsmen or public information custodians, a jurisdiction may have adopted the bully option.

Conclusion

Within organisations, employees can be subjected to the tactics of:

- blocking,
- spoiling,
- hurting, and,
- expulsion.

That experience can be imposed through the procedures of the organisation. The experience can be the product of the state of mind of an individual supervisor, or of an organisationally led control stratagem to ensure compliance by employees with a rogue solution to the problems of the organisation.

In the latter circumstances, the person who is a 'natural' at bullying has skills that meet the perceived needs of the organisation, particularly in the central PR/OD/HRM/CLO/EEO/IR functions and in its management teams. Thus organisational cultures are developed that are deeply ingrained with the problems bullying brings to organisational performance.

The consideration of 'bullying' within the context of individual bullies and individual victims does not expose the full harm that bully cultures bring to the effectiveness of organisations. The individual context encourages the bully problem to be seen as the province of the HRM manager. So it is, but only in small part.

In systemic bullying, the HRM office will have 'moon-faced men and red-dressed women'[1] already tested and selected for their skills in gatekeeping, and one or two will have experience in the support of higher forms of bullying, including expulsion.

It is only with an understanding of the *organisation as the bully* that full focus can be brought to bear on the disadvantages that bullying has for organisations. Then the scope of the task of recapturing organisational governance from bullies and their culture may be fully understood.

Note

1 A fitting caricature of human relations professionals provided by a colleague.

Bibliography

Fitzgerald, T (1989) *Report of a Commission of Inquiry Pursuant to Orders in Council into Possible Illegal Activities and Associated Police Misconduct* (29 June). Brisbane: Queensland Government.

Joint Standing Committee on Foreign Affairs, Defence and Trade (1999) *Military Justice Procedures in the Australian Defence Force* (June). Canberra: Department of Foreign Affairs, Defence and Trade.

Horngren, C and Foster, G (1987) *Cost Accounting: A Managerial Emphasis*. London: Prentice-Hall International.

Matthews, R (1994) *Report on its Public Hearings into the Improper Disposal of Liquid Waste in South East Queensland* (Vols 1 and 2, July and October). Brisbane: Criminal Justice Commission.

Morris, A and Howard, E (1999) *An Investigation into Allegations by Mr Kevin Lindeberg and Allegations by Mr Gordon Harris and Mr John Reynolds*. Brisbane: Queensland Government.

Queensland Government (1996–7) *Future Role, Structure, Powers, and Operations of the Criminal Justice Commission (Connolly/Ryan Inquiry)*. Brisbane: Queensland Government.

Senate Select Committee on Public Interest Whistleblowing (1994) *In the Public Interest.* Canberra: Parliament of Australia.

Chapter 7

The Reluctant Executioners

Vaughan Bowie

Only in fairy tales do we find pure heroes and unmitigated villains. In real life people are much more complex and unpredictable. In later life, I am finding it easier to forgive my enemies, because I am aware of the good they do alongside of the hurt they inflict.

(Yount, 1997: 78)

The nature of bad news infects the teller.

(*Anthony and Cleopatra*, Act 1, Scene 11)

The person who seeks revenge should dig two graves.

(Ancient proverb)

Introduction

Over the last two decades downsizing has become a common experience for many organisations and their employees. Dunphy and Griffiths (1998) note that over 3.3 million Australian employees were retrenched between 1996 and 1998. Supposed economic benefits have been the major drive underpinning this phenomenon. It has become apparent, however, that there have been great emotional, physical and financial costs for the 'victims' and survivors of this process. The focus of much of the current literature on downsizing has centred on these groups within organisations.

One group, however, that is often forgotten in this downsizing process is the middle-level management staff who are given the task of implementing the change process. Some managers may initially relish undertaking this task, but I suspect the majority are quite reluctant for a variety of reasons. As McKinley et al comment:

> [E]xecutives managing layoffs lie between a rock and a hard place. Without adequate severance pay, out placement services, and other forms of support to employees being laid off survivors will be alienated. On the other hand, support services to laid-off employees will increase costs. Either way costs mount, and managers find themselves engaging in repeated rounds of layoffs. (1995: 34)

This chapter outlines the physical, emotional and family 'cost' to managers involved in this process, and challenges many of the ideological assumptions underlying downsizing. Suggestions are then made as to alternative personal, managerial and organisational strategies that could be used to avoid or minimise the need for such drastic action.

The Executioners

Wright and Barling (1998) undertook research on a small quantitative sample of eight male and female 'executioners' from business and public service organisations in Canada. These managers had downsized anywhere from five to 100 employees. These managers had remarkably similar reactions to the processes in which they were involved.

The key effects they reported were that they found it professionally demanding, that it led to role overload, a search for some meaning in what they were doing, a sense of social and organisational isolation, a decrease in personal wellbeing and a decline in the quality of family life. Indeed, an examination of this research would suggest that most executioners could aptly be described as 'reluctant'. The following explores the themes emanating from this research in more detail.

Professionally demanding

Most participants commented that the task of downsizing was the most demanding task they had undertaken thus far in their professional lives. A number described how this process continued to have a long-term impact on them, even as long as 10 years after the event.

> Do not underestimate how profoundly this will affect you personally. And it is better to seek counselling earlier rather than later. You will need it. . . . This is something that can profoundly affect you. Many of your normal support networks fail. Friends and colleagues at work disappear very rapidly. (Wright and Barling, 1998: 341)

Some survey participants believed this process to be in direct contradiction to their normal participatory management style. Others commented that the skills they were learning in downsizing were not those required to initiate and maintain organisational development and growth. Many also expressed a fear that if downsizing could happen to others it could happen to them when their short-term usefulness to the organisation was finished.

Role overload

Wright and Barling (1998) quote research showing that as a result of downsizing, the remaining employees are undertaking 1.3 times as much work as a few years ago, doing more overtime, and taking fewer holidays or allowable paid leave. Indeed, those surveyed consistently said that the downsizing process led to a substantial increase in their workload both during and after the event.

> You need to change the time you commit to the job for two reasons. Number one because there is just as much [to do] and fewer people to do [it]. But number two is that psychologically you have to . . . the feeling is that you owe it to the people you let go to ensure that all their jobs get done. (Wright and Barling, 1998: 443)

Personal meaning

Another common theme of the research was that participants tried to find some purpose or meaning for their actions. As a whole the downsizers noted some measure of guilt about what they had done. One way some justified it to themselves was that this process did in fact rid the organisation of unproductive employees or the 'dead wood'. For some, however, this justification soon wore thin.

> I had to take out another group of people in December and it's emotionally draining because now what is happening is you get down to the meat and the fat is gone and you're taking out the worst of the best. (Wright and Barling, 1998: 345)

Others justified themselves in feeling that they had at least undertaken the process fairly and respected the dignity of the employees involved.

> I have the belief that you do this job the best you can. Individuals should be treated fairly by the organisation. I try to ensure that the decision process was fair and humanistic. I also try to provide the individual with a comfort structure. (Wright and Barling, 1998: 345)

Thus in the midst of such a bleak picture, those interviewed by Wright and Barling identified one small glimmer of hope:

> [T]hat hope is their own belief in how just they have been throughout the layoff process. Did they do everything possible to be fair in their deliberations, fair in their behaviour, and fair in their deeds? Armed with a justice defence, downsizers may be able to deflect some of the distress associated with this experience. If they felt they were fair in their actions and treated everyone honestly and honourably, downsizers might better be able to cope with the destructive nature of this experience. (Wright and Barling, 1998: 354)

The more conflictual the process, the greater the stress on the downsizers. There is some good evidence, as outlined by Brockner et al (1994), that if those who are downsized have a perception that they were dealt with fairly, that is, with procedural justice, their reactions are less negative than those who feel unjustly treated. Thus, the impact of this process on the executioners was greatly affected by the downsized employees' responses to the process.

Organisational and social isolation

As a result of the increased workload, guilt over the process, and the uncertainty and hostility of those who had so far survived the process, survey participants reported increasing isolation. To counter this isolation, downsizers turned to other downsizers outside the organisation for support. This process tended to further alienate them from their formal, social and family support networks. Thus, although downsizers described it as always a little lonely at the top, their involvement in the organisational downsizing increased this isolation.

Personal wellbeing

Many participants detailed the intense emotional, physical and behavioural pressure they were experiencing. Many referred to a direct link between the downsizing and a decline in their personal wellbeing.

> I know how painful this has been for me personally. I don't want this to happen again.
>
> . . .
>
> I mean I can't believe I survived that. It was horrible, just horrible. I really got concerned about my health, a couple of times I thought I was going to have a stroke and you have to remember . . . I was only 37 years old. (Wright and Barling, 1998: 349)

Frost and Robinson (1999: 98), in their research into what they call 'toxic handlers', interviewed 70 executives with similar roles to those of the executioners and outlined similar effects on their wellbeing:

> They often pay a steep price – professionally, psychologically, and sometimes physically. Some toxic handlers experience burnout; others suffer from far worse, such as ulcers and heart attacks.

Family wellbeing

Participants described a spill-over effect of the process on the extent and quality of their family interactions. This was a culmination of a combination of increased absence from home, emotional detachment when at home, not wishing to further burden their families and seeking support from other downsizers: 'The last four years have been very tough on myself and my family' (Wright and Barling, 1998: 350).

Wright and Barling (1998: 353) summarise the overall impact of this process as follows:

> Partially because of their choice and partially because of choices made by others, work for the downsizers becomes a lonely place. At home, because of unresolved conflicts, these individuals also tend to withdraw. Downsizers are tired: tired of the challenges at work and too tired to tackle problems at home. They are too tired to do anything much other than withdraw; in return, their closest companions respond in kind. . . . Without support at home, downsizers begin to experience an even deeper sense of social loneliness.

The following examines the same process in an Australian and personal context.

An Australian Experience

My current experience of downsizing has been in two areas, that of the human services, for example, health, welfare, youth and employment services, and that of higher education within the university sector. I have found myself in the position of being both a voluntary manager of a youth service whilst also an employee within a university. This process of downsizing in both the human services and higher education has often tended to pit the bosses and managers against the workers.

The management committee of this voluntary youth service on which I have served for 18 years moved last year towards a service restructure due to a lack of resources and unsatisfactory service delivery, which led us into an 'executioner' role. I observed in myself and other committee members the same frustration, stress and guilt reactions as identified by the 'reluctant executioners'. Finally, rather than confront this role head on, which would have meant a prolonged and bitter battle, the whole management committee resigned on mass.

In my other role as a university employee I have observed the impact of decisions to downsize on the deans, financial managers and teaching staff of such institutions. With increasing regularity, the threat of job losses if staff did not work harder and better, or return a larger financial contribution to the university, has distorted and, in many ways, decreased the quality of life and output of tertiary institutions.

Three years ago we gained several new deans with no previous loyalties to our university, whose briefs have been, amongst other tasks, to cut the financial expenditure in major ways because of increasing shortfalls in federal higher education funding. Such actions have led to job losses and the retrenchment of staff. A further irony has been that the most recent organisational restructuring has meant that the positions of these 'executioner' deans have in turn been restructured and their immediate future is most uncertain.

I have also watched with concern as senior academic staff with long histories within universities are being sidelined as they have refused or have not been able to make the hard financial decisions. From a distance I have also begun to observe a little of the emotional and psychological cost of downsizing on the downsizers.

How should we respond?

Ironically, recent research has begun to suggest that downsizing in its various forms has often not proven to be a good strategy for improving the economic wellbeing and performance of downsized organisations (Dunphy and Griffiths, 1998; McKinley et al, 1995; Wright and Smye, 1996).

Wayne Cascio (no date) outlines a number of myths associated with downsizing that need to be refuted. Let us look at some of these myths.

Myth 1: Downsizing boosts profits.
Reality: Companies' productivity after downsizing is quite mixed.

Myth 2: Downsizing is a last resort.
Reality: For many companies downsizing is a first resort.

Myth 3: Companies that are financially secure do not downsize.
Reality: Some financially secure companies with record profits are still downsizing.

Myth 4: Downsizing is a one off event for most companies.
Reality: The best predictor of whether a company will downsize is whether it has already downsized.

Myth 5: There are no adverse effects of downsizing on workload, morale or commitment to a company.
Reality: Downsizing does have a major negative impact on these factors within a company.

Thus, downsizing in itself as a long-term strategy is often just bad business. Even with this increasing realisation, the juggernaut of downsizing rolls on crushing many beneath its wheels in business, industry and the public service.

So how can we respond to this destructive process? Wright and Barling (1998) make only very limited suggestions about how we should respond. Their response basically acknowledges the process as a *fait accompli*, and these strategies are largely aimed at making the process as painless as possible for the workers and 'executioners' through better training and support for the staff implementing these changes. In contrast to this Cascio comments:

> Instead of asking, 'What's the irreducible core number of people we need to run our business?' responsible restructuring asks, 'How can we change the way we do business, so that we can use the people we have most effectively?' (p 15)

A range of possible responses can be made to the plight of the reluctant executioners who are placed in a very invidious position. Some are outlined below.

Do nothing

Our first response may be that they have got what they deserved and we should do nothing to help such people. We should therefore let them and their families suffer because of the choices the 'executioners' made. To say, 'I was only doing my job' may smack of the Nuremberg defence.

Understandably, if we have experienced a downsizing or the threat of it happening, this option may be as far as we are prepared to go at the moment. But what other options are there?

Increasing organisations' awareness of the negatives of downsizing

One strategy is to try to prevent the occurrence of this process in the first place. In many instances the decision to downsize has been made on incomplete or inaccurate information. As indicated by Wright and Smye (1996), the 'benefits' of this process may lead to short-term financial improvement and output. There is increasing evidence, however, questioning the long-term benefit of such moves at both the financial and staff morale levels. One ongoing strategy, then, should be keeping management and other key decision makers up to date with the current research on the impact of major organisational change and downsizing (see Dunphy and Griffiths, 1998).

McKinley et al (1995: 33) make extremely interesting observations as to why downsizing occurs in the first place. The core of their argument is that 'firms feel the pressure to downsize because being "lean and mean" has achieved the status of a valued attribute-and end in itself'. Their proposition is that the use of downsizing has little to do with its perceived economic benefits but occurs because of what they call constraining, cloning and learning.

> Constraining forces pressure organizations to confirm to institutional rules that define legitimate structures and management activities. . . . Cloning forces pressure organizations to mimic the actions of the most prestigious member of their industry. Finally, learning forces emerge through the management practices taught in universities or professional associations throughout the corporate world. (McKinley et al, 1995: 34)

They outline the four conditions that enhance the effects of constraining, cloning and learning on downsizing. These four are dependence, ambiguous performance standards, uncertain core technologies and frequent corporate interactions.

Dependence is the lemming-like quality of some organisations to copy their partners' or competitors' actions. Ambiguous performance standards refer to the difficulty in some organisations of judging outputs. Thus, if it is difficult to demonstrate the benefit of what you are doing you can at least demonstrate adherence to the dominant ideology of downsizing.

With uncertain core technologies it is not only unclear as to what the outputs are, as with the previous ambiguous standards, but also as to what the actual core skills are in the first place. McKinley et al comment:

> [T]echnological uncertainty helps explain why white collar workers and middle managers have taken big hits in recent episodes of corporate downsizing. These employees usually work with more uncertain technologies than blue-collar workers, and therefore they have been vulnerable to the bandwagon dynamics of downsizing in the 1990s. (1995: 38)

Frequency of interaction refers to the frequent contact between middle mangers from various organisations. McKinley et al explain it this way:

> Corporations that hire one another's executives, rub elbows at conferences, and use the same consultants, tend to learn one another's problems and solutions. This interaction promotes learning about how to downsize, and facilitates dissemination of the bright, attractive myths that make downsizing so compelling. (1995: 38)

Not surprisingly these authors then suggest that to reduce the external forces for downsizing, managers should reduce dependency, clarify performance standards, moderate technological uncertainty and disrupt standard interaction patterns.

Promote alternatives to downsizing

Closely related to the first strategy of raising awareness of the negative aspects of downsizing is to encourage exploration and promotion of other alternatives to this process (see Anfuso, 1996). This rationale could be based on the economic bottom line, but also on concepts of social capital and social responsibility.

Cascio suggests that rather than changing the number of people at work, changing the way the work is done is often the better approach and lists a number of ways this can be done, including increasing all the following:

- staff skills training and ongoing learning,
- information exchange,
- employee participation in the design and implementation of work processes,
- flattened organisational structures,

- worker–management partnerships,
- financial and other rewards linked to employee skills and performance,
- customer satisfaction as defined by customers.

He then goes on to give examples in a number of companies of strategies that have successfully incorporated these principles. The strategy options he suggests are:

- delaying without downsizing,
- changing organisational culture,
- employee involvement,
- employee buyouts,
- concessions for equity (employee partial stock ownership),
- employee exchanges,
- employee redeployment,
- voluntary leave of absence,
- downsizing without involuntary layoff, survivor training and education.

He concludes with what he calls guidelines for responsible restructuring, which should be read by any middle-level manager before they begin the 'execution' process. In many instances, if these guidelines were adhered to, most of this process would be unnecessary.

Resign

If the organisation wishes to proceed with the downsizing process the 'reluctant executioner' has the option to resign. As previously indicated, the management committee of which I was part, chose this option and 'fell on their sword'. Of course, in these days of increasing unemployment, especially amongst those in the middle-management level, this is an option not to be taken lightly.

Pass the task on to someone else

The 'executioner' could also attempt to 'pass the buck' and give the job to someone else, and therefore avoid direct responsibility for the task. There is often, however, a limited pool of 'executioners' within each organisation and avoidance of the task could count against a manager or supervisor later on and lead to their own early downsizing.

Provision of training and support for the process

Organisations themselves could provide some training and support for the downsizers either internally or externally. They could train their staff in how to implement this process humanely and ensure that procedural fairness was observed. If these services provided to the downsized employees minimised the impact on them, the secondary trauma felt by the 'executioners' might be lessened. Support could also be offered to the downsizers either through their employee assistance programs or through internal mechanisms.

Karl-Barry and Hancock (1999) outline some of the training that can be given to mangers involved in downsizing, but caution about the usefulness of some of the 'accepted wisdom' given in training about how, when and where such downsizings should take place. In smaller organisations, or where the downsizers do not have confidence in their organisation's support mechanisms, other external support structures may need to be found or developed. Frost and Robinson comment:

> Executives shouldn't count on support groups forming on their own, however, especially since most toxic handlers pride themselves on a high tolerance for personal pain . . . [b]etter, then, to suggest that the organization's toxic handlers meet with one another, and even arrange such meetings. And better yet to bring in experts who can guide toxic handlers through conversations that allow them to see, understand, and appreciate the pressures of what they do. (1999: 104)

Possibly the Beyond Bullying Association could be one of these support structures. Some may believe, however, there is an inherent contradiction or conflict of interest between the Association and downsizers.

Conclusion

Those of you reading this chapter who have been downsized or are facing this possibility may rightly respond with indignation and anger that I even consider some of the options raised above. I do not condone such behaviour but ask, 'Do we achieve anything from a sense of revenge or attempts to dehumanise the very ones that we feel may have dehumanised us?'

There is a quote from Aristotle (Goleman, 1996: ix) that goes something like this: 'Anyone can become angry – that is easy. But to be angry with the right person, to the right degree, at the right time, for the right purpose, and in the right way – this is not easy.' Diamond documents how this misdirected anger can polarise the workplace:

> [W]orkers' reactions to oppressive managerial practices often mirror the aggression of their superiors, closing a vicious circle of dominance and submission that virtually assures the continuation of an oppressive workplace. Workers, managers and executives often polarise into subgroups that view the other as 'all bad' (evil and punishing) and themselves as 'all good' (righteous and victimized). (1997: 10)

Is the 'story', however, as simple as the guys in the white hats ('us') versus the bad guys in the black hats ('them')? Or is it as Yount (1997) suggested in the opening quote to this chapter that staff at all levels of organisations have mixed motives for what they do and how they react. I believe the latter is the case. Lloyd reflects this approach in his comments:

> We must recognize that our vested interests are tied to one another and only through recognizing and responding to those interests on multiple levels can we jointly build credibility, security, and accomplishments toward any number of outcomes. (Williams, 1994: 18)

So if we are angry or threatened, how can we express this energy in the most constructive way for positive change that does not destroy us or the 'reluctant executioners', whilst at the same time taking collective action to stop the downsizing juggernaut? I have only very partial and fragmented answers to these questions as already suggested. I do know, however, as suggested by Aristotle, that we need to be more constructive in our use of our anger and not expend it incorrectly or in an unfocused manner.

I believe our energies should be focused on the dominant ideology behind the discredited 'theory' of downsizing – that of economic (ir)rationalism. It is this ideology that gives power to misguided small elites to manipulate both middle-level managers and workers in a dehumanising way for the 'benefit' of the market and a group of rich shareholders and power brokers.

I will end with a short poem from Yeats (Finneran, 1996) called 'The Great Day':

> Hurrah for the revolution and more cannon shot!
> A beggar on horseback lashes a beggar on foot.
> Hurrah for the revolution and cannon come again!
> The beggars have changed places but the lash goes on.

What will we do if we ever get onto the horse?

References

Anfuso, D (1996) 'Saving Jobs: Strategies to Stop Layoffs' 73 *Personnel Journal* 66–77.

Brockner, J, Konovosky, M, Cooper-Schneider, R, Folger, R, Martin, C and Bies, R (1994) 'Interactive Effects of Procedural Justice and Outcome Negativity on Victims and Survivors of Job Loss' 37(2) *Academy of Management Journal* 575–80.

Cascio, W (nd) 'The Guide to Responsible Restructuring', at <http://www.mgmt.utoronto.ca/~evans/teach363/downsize/respes.htm>.

Diamond, M (1997) 'Administrative Assault: A Contemporary Psychoanalytic View of Violence and Aggression in the Workplace' 27(3) *American Review of Public Administration* 228–48.

Dunphy, D and Griffiths, A (1998) *The Sustainable Corporation: Organizational Renewal in Australia.* Sydney: Allan & Unwin.

Finneran, R (ed) (1996) *The Collected Poems of WB Yeats* (2nd edition, revised). New York: Scribner.

Frost, P and Robinson, S (1999) 'The Toxic Handler Organizational Hero: And Casuality' *Harvard Business Review* (July–August) 99–106.

Goleman, D (1996) *Emotional Intelligence.* London: Bloomsbury.

Karl-Barry, A and Hancock, W (1999) 'Expert Advice on Employment Termination Practice: How Expert is it?' 28(1) *Public Personnel Management* 56–62.

McKinley, W, Sanchez, C and Schick, A (1995) 'Organizational Downsizing: Constraining, Cloning, Learning' 9(3) *Academy of Management Executive* 32–44.

Williams, L (1994) *Organizational Violence.* Westport, CT: Quorum Books.

Wright, B and Barling, J (1998) '"The Executioners' Song": Listening to the Downsizers Reflect on Their Experiences' 14(4) *Canadian Journal of Administrative Science* 339–355.

Wright, L and Smye, M (1996) *Corporate Abuse: How 'Lean and Mean' Robs People and Profits.* Toronto: Key Porter Books.

Yount, D (1997) *Spiritual Simplicity.* New York: Simon & Schuster.

Chapter 8

Epiphany

A Method of Analysis for Workplace Violence

Fiona Underwood

This chapter attempts to portray the realm of workplace violence. For some who experience violence, the meaning of the incident manifests itself in a turning point, a critical incident (Sikes et al, 1985) or peak moment (Maslow, 1970) or, as termed here, as an epiphany (Denzin, 1989). The use of epiphany in literature traverses many fields including fiction, religion, psychology and education. My intention in this chapter is to provide a snapshot of a qualitative investigation into workplace violence, and with this focus I shall explore how the notion of epiphany can be used to assist in producing a greater understanding of meanings in interview texts about workplace violence in the Supported Accommodation Assistance Program (SAAP) sector.

Workplace Violence

Inordinate power differentials in the workplace have been framed as both workplace bullying (McCarthy et al, 1996; Thompson, 1998; Zapf, 1999) and workplace violence (Bowie, 1989; Rayner and Hoel, 1997; Rey, 1996; WorkCover, 1996; 1997). As this chapter does not intend to resolve the debate about the meaning of workplace bullying and violence,[1] I will use them interchangeably here. At this point Denzin's definition of violence is helpful, as 'the attempt to regain, through the use of emotional and physical force, something that has been lost' (1984: 488).

In addition, feminist perspectives of violence have shown that women are less likely to experience physical violence but more likely to experience sexual violence and verbal abuse (Hamner and Saunders, 1984;

Stanko, 1985). After acknowledging the slipperiness of these notions I now to turn to the context of the investigation.

The SAAP Context

The residential community service of the Supported Accommodation Assistance Program (SAAP), established by the Commonwealth government in 1985, consists of social workers, welfare para-professionals, and refuge and related workers. Workers' safety in the SAAP sector has been described by Bowie:

> These workplaces have a high potential for violent incidents. Current research seems to indicate a trend toward increasing numbers of violent incidents against human service workers. . . . [C]lients are often stressed, angry, hostile and may be under the influence of drugs or alcohol. Some have serious behaviour problems and psychiatric illnesses. (WorkCover, 1996: 4)

Whilst workplace violence for SAAP staff has been addressed in terms of prediction and prevention of violent episodes in the SAAP sector (Squire, 1997), the meaning of experiencing workplace violence for staff in SAAP services does not appear to have been investigated from a qualitative perspective. This is a sensitive topic to investigate. By referring to Bowie's observations on the SAAP context above, it could be construed that young people in SAAP services are the only source of violence towards staff. On the contrary, this chapter will illustrate that workplace violence perpetuated by management is also a feature of the SAAP sector.

The Study

My interpretative research so far consists of 28 open-ended interviews with workers and managers of SAAP services. I have sought from these participants their definitions of workplace violence, rich descriptions of what it means to them and accounts of what they have learnt from any experiences of workplace violence they may have had while working in SAAP services. In the process of collecting this qualitative material, several participants have shared stories of their life experiences that have radically altered meanings they held about themselves (Denzin, 1989). It is here that the qualitative perspective is further defined by applying 'epiphany' as a method of analysis for one selected interview.

Epiphany as a Method of Analysis

The notion of epiphany has an extensive history. In religious terms epiphany is understood to be the manifestation of Jesus Christ (*Epiphania*)

(Baldovin, 1987: 132). However, since the Roman liturgy has become widely dominant, most Western Christians understand epiphany as 'the Feast of the Magi', a symbolic reference of Christ's manifestation to the gentiles (ibid: 132). As a major baptismal day for Eastern Christians it was named in Greek *Ta Phota* ('the lights'), whilst baptism was referred to as *Photismos* ('enlightenment') (ibid: 132). It is these understandings (the manifested knowledge and enlightened awareness) that are borrowed from the religious notion of epiphany and applied to the qualitative approach for this investigation of the meanings of workplace violence.

As Maslow states, 'the theological literature has generally assumed an absolute, qualitative difference between the mystic experience and all others' (1970: 164). By removing the supernatural references, it is possible to make plausible claims about varying intensities of the experience and to suggest different meanings for them. The similarities between critical incidents and the epiphany generated by qualitative inquiry are found in the educationalist literature (Woods, 1994). Likewise, from fiction Denzin has borrowed from James Joyce's work the notion of epiphany 'to describe those interactional moments that leave positive and negative marks on people's lives' (1989: 125). What is characteristic of all of these perspectives is the interactionist view informing the knowledge that epiphanic experiences generate. Further, Denzin explains epiphany as specific to his method of interpretative interactionism as follows: in epiphanies 'personal character is manifested and made apparent. By recording these experiences in detail, the researcher is able to illuminate the moments in crisis that occur in a person's life' (1989: 15).

Several studies have used the notion of an epiphany for a method of analysis for interpreting text. In nursing literature epiphanic knowledge is understood to be those moments when one 'sees familiar things in a fresh light' (Hawkins in Howe, 1994: 275). In an inquiry into women's subjective experiences of learning they are HIV-infected, the meaning of these experiences was patterned as epiphany, confirmation and calamity. The epiphanies produced by the HIV diagnosis 'turned on a light', producing insights that inspired radical changes for some women (Stevens and Doerr, 1997: 529).

In my investigation epiphany is further identified by the pattern of several elements that point to the experience, the crisis moment, the turning point and the outcomes of the experience – the new or changed shape in meaning (Denzin, 1989). This pattern will be shown to revolve around a metaphor framing the meaning of an experience of violence in the selected interview text for this chapter.

By framing Jan's (a pseudonym) story as an epiphany I attempt to illuminate a wider political, social interpretation that is contained in her biographical tale (Denzin, 1997). For the reader I then offer an understanding of what the working conditions of the SAAP sector can entail and point to the need for attention to worker safety in this human service industry.

Illuminating the Epiphany

The following extracts are from one interview where Jan discusses her experiences of workplace violence caused by a manager over a period of eight years. This occurs in what Jan describes as a '24-hour intensive shelter for young people under the age of 18', which has several managers in a large non-government organisation that houses an SAAP service. What is remarkable about this case is the fact that these workers, who throughout most of this ordeal felt isolated, as individual victims of their manager's bullying, not only survived this workplace violence, but survived it by uniting together to take action. This team sought not only to address the manager's inappropriate behaviour, but also to confront the issues of organisational culture that had permitted the manager's unacceptable behaviour to continue and escalate over this lengthy period of time. While the text speaks volumes, the analysis is selective in order to highlight the emergence of the constructed epiphany.

The Epiphanic Crisis

We start with Jan describing how she felt about these experiences of hierarchical workplace violence.

Jan: Okay, what I was just going to say about the clients, that I was just going to say the worst – the worst abuse, was from our [manager].

Jan: And it just went on and on. It got to the point where I wouldn't go to any meetings where he would be.

Jan: And it was almost like a domestic violence . . . situation as well, where you are . . . ashamed. You know, well, you blame yourself for a while, so I must have done something wrong. And so then you try and make him happy. But then you realise it doesn't matter what you do, it's him!

Jan's language shows a rather sophisticated understanding of violence – an understanding of some emotional characteristics (shame and self-blame) that have been found to be common to domestic violence and child abuse experiences. Yet although she has this comprehension of the notion, Jan describes her experience of the phenomenon by first attributing responsibility for the occurrence of violence to herself. This fits with much of the feminist literature on domestic violence, whereby women often attribute the cause of male violent behaviour to themselves and make efforts to appease a male for relief from violence or violent threats. Jan goes on to describe further emotional and physical reactions to this experience of workplace violence perpetuated by one of her managers.

Jan: But is was just wrong and it was making me sick.

Fiona: Sure.

Jan: I was – I was in, you know . . . I had heart palpitations; I had gastro; I had diarrhoea. It was becoming very physical. And I also felt very guilty. We had these managers' meetings once a week. And I felt, um, that when someone got picked on in meetings, I felt good that it wasn't me. And afterwards I felt very guilty that we didn't support each other.

Fiona: Right.

Jan: But, um, there was nothing we could do. It was the link that we might be attacked.

Fiona: So how did you cope with that?

Jan: We had counselling. But we were terrified – we were terrified of this man. I use to think he was going to come here and shoot us or something. I was really scared, really scared!

In this above text Jan's language also suggests the isolation that she felt through these experiences. This is hinted at here with her mention of the link, a symbolic link embedded with contradictory meaning. It was the common element that she shared with her other colleagues in this experience – the shared fear of being attacked, which also appears to have served to maintain their isolation from one another for a lengthy period of time, perhaps a number of years. Jan's complex understanding of violence is further demonstrated in the disclosure of her own emotions of feeling good, then feeling guilty when threats were made by this manager. These feelings are reiterated in the following passage.

Jan: Right, I am a very peace-loving person you see, and I am very much a pacifist. I don't like violence of any sort. And so I find violence simply very scary, very threatening, very uncomfortable. I am not the sort of person to scream back or yell back. I'm not like that. I try to work with kids in a very gentle way. I don't believe that we should have power over the kids or anything else.

Fiona: Sure.

Jan: So I guess in some ways it's reaffirming that what I am doing is right. But I wish I had more guts in some ways; I am still feeling bad about my colleagues in that situation. Because [if] we [had] stuck together we could have done something about it earlier.

In these extracts above, Jan's character is further revealed through her narrative of what it meant to experience this violence. The meaning of her defined peace-loving nature is made apparent with reference to her work with her SAAP residents. The complexity of this trait is revealed in her apparent desire to have had more strength of character, which may have helped her deal with the violence in a more productive way.

The Turning Point

Whilst division and isolation seemed common amongst SAAP staff, the text below highlights a turning point.

Jan: And we got together and fought and so all our staff, everyone, stuck together – it was absolutely incredible.

Fiona: And what was the turning point there again, that brought you together?

Jan: It was that someone spoke to the Occupational Health and Safety Officer and it got back to [senior management]. And then they started to ask questions. And once they started to ask questions we thought, hey, you know, we could tell the truth about whatever happened.

Fiona: Okay, and so it was that process that started to unify everyone?

Jan: And we all got together and joined the union and we got legal help and everything – it was great, it was *really good*, it was a really positive thing to do after however many years of being victims. And the weird thing is that we are all very intelligent. We are good at what we do. We're good at our job, educated – the whole thing – and we were just like pathetic bits of quivering jelly. Amazing.

In the above text, my question about the turning point for these episodes of workplace violence may be seen to be leading the construction of the awareness of workplace violence. However, it is here I argue that the spontaneous metaphor of 'quivering bits of jelly' holds the key to this text's truth. This metaphor, which contrasted with her pride in the efforts of her teamwork to redress the violence, indicates the emerging epiphany for Jan. In the extract below, the issue arises of applying learning received from training to the ongoing experiences of management violence, and it gives important insight to the meaning of the metaphor 'quivering bits of jelly'.

Fiona: Okay, so that is training for workplace violence in the workplace. And we [were] talking about your having some stress management. Did the bulk of this training happen while this particular staff member was still here?

Jan: Oh yeah, yeah.

Fiona: And how did you find . . . ?

Jan: Well, no one talked about it. This was the funny thing. It was happening to everyone. Everyone knew it was happening to them, but everyone was terrified of him, but no one said, 'This is violent.' It was never, 'This is not acceptable behaviour', 'This is not on', this is just . . . [the violent manager].

It appears in this text that Jan did not perceive the training as applicable to the violence or bullying perpetrated by her manager before her team took collective action. There could be numerous reasons for this. For example, it could be that the training was not appropriate for their experiences, perhaps targeting clients rather than management. Another possibility is that the power of the manager was so overwhelming for these people that they did not believe the training would have a beneficial impact if put into practice. In this context of apparent non-transference of learning from training for workplace violence, Jan offers the metaphor of boiling frogs to help explain the episodes of workplace violence for these workers.

The Epiphanic Metaphor

Jan: It's like frogs really. You get a frog and throw it into a pot of boiling water and it will jump out. . . . If you put it in there and you heat it up gradually, it will cook before you know it. And that's what happened with us. So we didn't actually see this violence until, until we were way out of it, and we thought this was not okay, what was going on.

Fernandez helps explain the importance of metaphor for qualitative understanding:

> Metaphor . . . is the statement of an association between things that are normally categorised in separate domains of experience. This association cannot be based on designative or literal defining features but rather on the figurative or connotative features the two things have in common. (1986: 176)

ively, the metaphor of frogs thrown into boiling water can be od to be a most violent act against living beings. Used here the metaphor conjures up the image of the workers experiencing gradually increasing violence, and, like the frogs in water slowly heated to boiling point, not becoming aware of their parlous situation. It is a powerful metaphor when we recognise that metaphors are used to fill gaps created by the inadequacies of literal language (Fernandez, 1986: 178). Furthermore, I argue that the power of metaphors are apparent when they are created in those spontaneous moments when one is desperate for language to capture and convey the importance of the meaning of the lived experience in question. This metaphor of the boiling frogs has all these elements. The meaning of the metaphor is further illustrated in Jan's discussion below about the relevance of training.

Fiona: Right, sure, sure. So you weren't recognising it, until . . . ?

Jan: No.

Fiona: And so the training that you were having . . . ?

Jan: Didn't, yeah, it didn't register, that this is about this – [it's] applicable. But even if you tried to be assertive with him or anything else it would only get worse, I mean, you couldn't change him at all. If he said everything was purple with green spots, you would say, 'Yes.' . . . Which was really sad.

Fiona: This is an extraordinary . . .

Jan: Yeah, and I promise you it's all true. And I promise you that it is probably, I mean, it was just continual. Habitual abuse.

Fiona: Did you want to say more about that?

Jan: No, it was just a nightmare. And people knew it. People higher up than he was, knew what he was like, and no one helped us. . . . No one helped us.

And further along in the interview Jan offers an explanation of why other workers may not have helped the staff who experienced this violence.

Jan: I think they think we are a nuisance, still. I think that, unfortunately, well, not unfortunately, but the majority of us are women and I think they think it's just, you know, women's stuff. Um, I think they know it's true and they believe us, but they think that we are overreacting. They probably think that, I mean, they did something about it in the end. I don't hate them for that.

Fiona: Yes.

Jan: But, they all knew what was happened and they just ignored it.

Jan's description of organisational response to this manager's violence raises the need for a feminist perspective of violence. Jan's language is clearly suggesting here that perhaps the way other organisational staff dealt with these stories of workplace violence was to use a gendered interpretation, which subjugated the women's experience, thereby denying the validity of these experiences, and the effect of which was perhaps to prolong the resolution of the episodes of violence.

Epiphanic Outcome

The following text is the postscript to the interview. I had turned off the tape after we had concluded the interview. However, Jan continued to say more about the meaning of the workplace violence. I therefore asked if she would repeat this for the purpose of capturing her text on tape. It narrates the changes that have occurred in this work context since this extraordinary collective experience of workplace violence was resolved.

Jan: Okay, just saying that with the team leaders and things now we keep really open communication. And if [we] hear something, that someone has been talking about you, we actually ring each other up on the telephone and talk about it. Because we actually found that prior to [the manager] leaving, that often we were set up against each other. And so our energy was actually directed against our colleagues instead of [against] the person it should have been directed [against].

What is also of interest about this case study is that other workers who were interviewed in this SAAP agency did not leave the agency. All workers did unite to address the workplace violence and sought to have the perpetrator of the violence – the manager in question – removed. This outcome is in contrast to many others where violence is involved, where the victim often finds they are the one who needs to move from the context of violence in an effort to stop the violence against them.

Conclusion

In an effort to create a new way of understanding the meaning of workplace violence I have constructed an epiphany out of Jan's text. This entailed the epiphanic elements of a crisis, a turning point and an outcome.

In summary, these elements were created out of her reflections on the domestic violence traits she identified in her experiences of workplace violence, including her feeling bad and guilty about the lack of support she provided her colleagues through the episodes of manager violence, constituting what I suggest is the epiphanic crisis. Her description of the contact with the occupational health and safety officer, joining the union, getting legal help and uniting with her colleagues and being able to *tell the truth* about what happened, is what I frame as the epiphanic turning point. The epiphanic outcome I suggest is contained in Jan's story of how she is now conscious of clear open communication with her colleagues to prevent their being set up against each other again through isolation and silence as a strategy of workplace violence used by others. Further, the value of the metaphor of the boiling frogs is useful in representing denial of workplace violence and non-transference of adult learning to the workplace.

On a closing note, while Jan's text is full of multivoice constructions of meaning that are all subject to different readings, this chapter has endeavoured to illustrate how an epiphany can form a method of analysis useful for portraying meanings in stories of workplace violence. I argue that it has value for us when we are able to gain more insightful knowledge about the meanings of workplace violence through these constructions, such as the need for more attention to workers' conditions and ways of surviving workplace violence in the SAAP sector.

Note

Many thanks to Dr Susan Howard, Senior Lecturer, University of South Australia, for her valuable comments on the preparation of this article.

1 Indeed Bessant and Cook (1998: 13) argue that bullying, due to its discrete, often indirect and systematic nature, often means it is embedded in and legitimised through custom, language and law, which leads to the invisibility of it rather than producing social recognition and response to it as a form of violence. Further, they argue the language of bullying and harassment may even weaken the meaning of the word 'violence'. I would add that this view seems somewhat contrary to the emerging research in this field and to the views aired in the Australian media on the notion of workplace bullying over the past 18 months.

References

Baldovin, J (1987) 'Epiphany', in M Eliade (ed), *The Encyclopedia of Religion*, vol 5. New York: Macmillan, pp 132–3.

Bessant, J and Cook, S (1998) 'The Sovereign State and Obligations to Protect Women against Violence' 13 *Just Policy* 10–19.

Bowie, V (1989) *Coping with Violence*. Sydney: Karibuni Press.

Denzin, N (1984) 'Toward a Phenomenology of Domestic, Family Violence' 90 *American Journal of Sociology* 483–513.

Denzin, N (1989) *Interpretative Interactionism*. Newbury Park, CA: Sage.

Denzin, N (1997) *Interpretative Ethnography: Ethnographic Practices for the 21st Century*. Thousand Oaks, CA: Sage.

Fernandez, J (1986) 'The Argument of Images and the Experience of Returning to the Whole', in V Turner and E Bruner (eds), *The Anthropology of Experience*. Champaign, IL: University of Illinois Press.

Hamner, J and Saunders, S (1984) *Well Found Fear: A Community Study of Violence to Women*. London: Hutchinson, in association with the Explorations in Feminism Collective.

Howe, E (1994) 'Some Prices of Epiphany and the Occasional Need to Stigmatise Patients to Offset Them' 5(4) *Journal of Clinical Ethics* 275–82.

McCarthy, P, Sheehan, M and Wilkie, W (1996) *Bullying: From Backyard to Boardroom*. Sydney: Millennium.

Maslow, A (1970) *Motivation and Personality*. New York: Harper & Row.

Rayner, C and Hoel, H (1997) 'Workplace Violence: Cause for Concern or the Construction of a New Category of Fear' 39(1) *Journal of Industrial Relations* 21–32.

Rey, L (1996) 'What Social Workers Need to Know about Client Violence' 77(1) *Family in Society: The Journal of Contemporary Human Services* 33–9.

Squire, R (ed) (1997) *Supported Accommodation Assistance Program Newsletter* (May). Canberra: Commonwealth Department of Health and Family Services.

Sikes, P, Measor, L and Woods, P (1985) *Teacher Careers: Crisis and Continuities*. Lewes: Falmer Press.

Stanko, E (1985) *Intimate Intrusions: Women's Experiences of Male Violence*. London: Unwin & Hyman.

Stevens, P and Doerr, T (1997) 'Trauma of Discovery: Women's Narratives of Being Informed they are HIV-infected' 9(5) *AIDS CARE* 523–38.

Thompson, C (1998) *Workplace Bullying Project*. Adelaide: Working Women's Centre of SA, WorkCover and SA Health Commission Health Promotion Unit.

Woods, P (1994) 'Collaborating in Historical Ethnography: Researching Critical Events in Education' 7(4) *Qualitative Studies in Education* 309–21.

WorkCover (1996) *Preventing Violence in the Accommodation Services of the Social and Community Services Industry*. Sydney: Department of Community Services (NSW) and WorkCover NSW.

WorkCover (1997) 'Claims for Community Services and Violence in the Workplace' (1991–2 and 1996–7). Adelaide: WorkCover.

Zapf, D (1999) '*Mobbing in Organisationen: Ein Überblick zum Stand der Forschung*' ['Mobbing in organisations: A state-of-the-art research review'] 43 *Zeitschrift für Arbeits- und Organisationspsychologie* 1–25.

Chapter 9

The Bullying Syndrome

Complicity and Responsibility

Paul McCarthy

Introduction

Threats to identity and esteem, and fears of job loss have been a feature of workplaces reconfiguring in the interests of survival and profit in globalisation in the 1990s. The ferment of distress at work and wider socio-economic *fears of falling* (Ehrenreich, 1990) provide a potent context for the construction of *bullying-at-work* as a syndrome. Here, 'syndrome' is used to describe convergence in meanings across disciplines and in the public domain, leading to more common ways of describing symptoms and causes of distress, and prescribing remedies. For example, chronic fatigue, gulf war, recovered memory and multiple personality have been identified as syndromes by Showalter (1997). Mutual recognition of unreasonable behaviours and their effects, and the need for remedies, among professionals and employees in organisations undergoing continuous change feature in the recent development of understandings of bullying at work as a syndrome.

The rise of concern about bullying in Australian workplaces reflects international trends (Adams, 1992; Leymann, 1996; Nicarthy et al, 1993). The 1994 conference, Beyond Bullying: Towards National Guidelines, represented a significant local manifestation of these concerns. The conference was promoted by the then newly formed Brisbane-based Beyond Bullying Association (BBA). That conference effectively established bullying, hitherto a school-centred notion in Australia, as a signifier of behaviours contributing to distress in the workplace. The genesis of the BBA can be seen in widespread story-telling and sharing of concerns about distress at work – in social interaction, in counselling, in medical and legal consultations, and in public, educational and research forums.

The BBA then networked its concerns with the Queensland Working Women's Service (QWWS), who developed profiles of client experiences of bullying, advice on remedies, and counselling and referral services. Several conferences, public forums, publications and widespread media attention involving the BBA and QWWS followed. In 1997, QWWS lead the formation of a working party to develop industry self-regulation guidelines, resulting in the release of *Workplace Bullying: An Employer's Guide* (Division of Workplace Health and Safety: 1998).

In 2001, the *Guide* is arguably becoming a dominant discourse for the explanation and remedy of distress at work stemming from unreasonable behaviours. Here, 'discourse' is used in a Foucauldian sense, to signify shared ways of understanding a phenomenon at a particular time, through meanings arising at the intersection of a number of disciplinary ways of seeing (Fillingham, 1993).

The psychological potency of bullying, as a lightning rod or a solar collector of distress and resentments in contemporary Australian workplaces has enabled the diffusion of the discourse of bullying at work (DBW). Widespread attribution of causes of distress at work to bullying is now evident in original Australian research findings (McCarthy et al, 1995; Thompson, 1998). In addition, the 1998 QWWS annual report evidenced bullying as the greatest source of complaints about workplace experiences. They represented 27% of enquires, up from 10% in 1995. The terminology has also spread through therapeutic, industrial, employee assistance, occupational health and safety, legal, and management practice.

My aim is to investigate implications for responsibility stemming from the construction of DBW. Here, 'responsibility' is defined in terms of rights, duties and obligations, such as those expressed in codes of ethics in workplaces and in civil society, and also in ethics resulting from sharing concerns with others, particularly in less powerful social groups. The approach taken models DBW as a syndrome in Showalter's (1997) terms, and maps the relations of desire and complicity for those variously taking the positions of the professional (therapeutic-managerial authority), bully or victim in the discourse. An understanding of these relations is considered a necessary step in addressing issues of responsibility.

In examining DBW as a syndrome, I seek to respect the integrity and dignity of victims, yet considers the approach is justified because uncritical adoption of its meanings could further perpetuate cycles of victimisation. My overriding concern is that, whilst victim-identity can be empowering and bring into play much needed interventions, identity ascribed by DBW can be doubly victimising at its limits. This is particularly the case, if following *the way of DBW* in good faith compounds stress and leaves victims worse off, for example, through:

- seeking remedies by a victim that results in their being excluded from paid work;
- applications to tribunals or courts that endure for several years, leaving victims financially and emotionally impoverished;
- constructions of perpetrators that distract attention from more removed power holders responsible for unconscionable behaviours and impossible pressures resulting in bullying;
- risks of action for negligence as a consequence of inappropriate problem diagnosis and intervention; and
- approaches that diminish the need for wider community activism, workplace activism, and political activism to challenge the structures in thought, organisations and society that transmit bullying and maintain the victim's status.

The Bullying Syndrome

Throughout history, distress commonly experienced in everyday life has been constructed as syndromes by professionals in the service of a public anxiously seeking remedies. History is also replete with examples of dangers of less than critical constructions of syndromes by vested interest groups, and their willing adoption by publics. These dynamics are eloquently addressed in Showalter's (1997) analysis of the social construction of syndromes as giving meaning to distress. Showalter's findings suggest that modelling a discourse such as DBW as a syndrome is an exercise of intellectual responsibility. This responsibility lies in the interests of identifying limits, or points at which further disadvantage could unwittingly be inflicted on victims in following meanings and remedies, both implicit and explicit within the discourse.

Importantly, Showalter does not regard the multiplicity of expressions of distress, emotionality and hysteria as a consequence of disturbing experiences as 'weakness, badness, feminine deceitfulness, or irresponsibility, but rather as a cultural symptom of anxiety and stress'. Furthermore, she sees conflicts producing the symptoms as 'genuine and universal', continuing that victims are 'not liars' and therapists are 'not villains', rather that the syndromes are constructed by 'suffering patients, caring psychologists, dedicated clergy, devoted parents, hardworking police, concerned feminists and anxious communities'. She also considers that therapeutic interventions are absolutely necessary if a person is to remain functional (Showalter, 1997: 9).

Contentiously, Showalter locates these assemblages – distress, psychosomatic expression and syndrome-construction – within the history of hysteria. With relief, hysteria plays some part in everyday life emotionality for all of us – 'we are all hysterics especially when we are writing papers' (1997: 15). Also, Showalter suggests that 'redefining hysteria as [a] universal human response to emotional conflict is a better course than evading, denying, or projecting its realities' (1997: 17). In the parallel reading of Showalter's *Hystories* (1997) and DBW, we are alerted to ways distress experienced at work is socially constructed as bullying in DBW, and to the responsibilities to which that gives rise.

Common syndrome construction processes noted by Showalter include: circulation of experiences causing panic through stories, the media, and dialogues with professionals able to name symptoms; expression of feelings as a form of social communication of inexpressible feelings and as part of the healing process; naming that legitimises the victim's malaise and accords authority to the diagnostician; and 'social and cultural recruitment' as distressed individuals respond to the stereotypes (1997: 18, 19). Arguably, from a critical perspective, dynamics of the social construction of DBW bear some similarity to these processes.

In addition, a historical lineage of negative stereotyping and feminising of experienced emotional distress is brought to our attention by Foucault. Foucault demonstrates how therapies for 'dysfunctional' emotionality can be located in a long history of the hystericisation of women's bodies by the medical profession. Showalter identifies mutuality in this process, observing that '[d]octors needed hysterical women as muses, and hysterical women needed doctors to speak for them' (1997: 19). However, in the contours of 'culturally permissible expressions of distress' male hysteria has traditionally been denied, as a consequence of 'avoidance, suppression and disguise' (1997: 13, 64).

Arguably, DBW could be seen as a new moment in this lineage, emerging from a new trajectory in which the male body-at-work is downshifted, downsized, restructured, feminised and hystericised. DBW makes his stories of distress at work possible as an outcome of a sharing of experiences at work between men and women, and with the help of women's experience in finding voices to address male violence. Indeed, the 'private, secret, insidious traumas' given voice in feminist analysis (Showalter, 1997: 61) resonate strongly with experiences of bullying at work reported by both men and women. DBW now models conditions in which therapeutic authorities may speak for males traumatised in the pressures of restructuring, and allows professionals to illustrate and valorise their practices in relation to male distress-at-work.

Modelling DBW in these terms suggests the need to open space for critical reflection on the process of its construction as a syndrome and on the ways people give meanings to the distress of bullying. Of course, one may choose meanings other than those in DBW. A prototype for the resistance of syndrome meanings may be found in Showalter's reading of Freud's case Dora, where Dora's resources enabled her to resist and disconnect from the victim-identity imposed by Freud's narrative (1997: 44). Showalter's re-reading suggests we can learn to retell experiences in ways that overcome victim-identities that are regressive, infantile, or stuck in revenge (1997: 205). The value of writing, speaking, and activism in transcending hysteria as a consequence of culturally imposed silence is also demonstrated in feminist reinterpretations of Freud's case Anna O (Showalter, 1997: 58).

Not facing the 'hidden fantasies, myths, and anxieties' in the social construction of syndromes poses dangers for both professionals and victims. Possibilities of damage arise, 'in distracting us from the real problems and crises of modern society, in undermining respect for evidence and truth, and in helping to support an atmosphere of conspiracy and suspicion' (Showalter, 1997: 206–7).

Limits of Bullying at Work: Desire, Complicity and Responsibility

The following discussion explores the limits of meanings generated amongst three key actors in the discourse of bullying at work (DBW), namely professional, bully, and victim. Any discussion of desire and complicity in DBW is highly contentious, and risks furthering a masculine 'blame the victim' approach to those experiencing distress. However, not discussing relations of desire and complicity at all points in the professional–bully–victim triangle risks leaving dynamics of power enabling bullying to remain unexamined.

The notion of 'desire' used in the following discussion signifies processes through which embodied bio-psycho-socio-politico interests are invested in taking a position in the meanings of DBW. Furthermore, 'complicity' is seen to occur through trade-offs of survival needs, satisfactions and costs at the moment of exchange wherein desire recognises itself in DBW, and the discourse validates and attributes meaning to experience. Complicity may well arise from the expression of desire in terms of DBW because there is no other recourse in a person's life-world, as is common in deregulated and male-dominated environments.

Following are several cameo simulations of the relations of desire and complicity that exist on tangents that variously enable and constrain DBW. The writer aims to flag limitations of the discourse by identifying silences and contradictions that risk compounding victimisation as well as by raising issues of responsibility.

Resistance

Distress at work in the 1990s, as a consequence of organisational restructuring, resonates with political bullying by both major parties that occurred throughout the 1990s. Thus, it was evident in brutal parliamentary banter and economic rationalist policies. Profiteering from the pain of restructuring in the accrual of short-term downsizing gains to immediate shareholders and highly paid executives, related threats of job-loss and social dislocation, and high unemployment, all contributed to the ferment giving rise to DBW.

Political expression of resentments to bullying at work causing distress has remained frustrated. Both Labor and Coalition parties have subscribed to callous economic rationalism, and smaller parties have not taken on bullying as an issue. Some of these resentments have been collected within the ambit term *bullying* in a community network, and relayed into action for change. What has occurred in Brisbane exemplifies this. From modest initial psychological and academic interests in Brisbane, the network has expanded through the BBA and QWWS, the Australian Institute of Management (Qld), and the Queensland Chamber of Commerce and Industry, as well as employee assistance providers, health services, unions, support groups, psychiatrists, counsellors, educators, academics and lawyers. Understanding the activism driving DBW helps us appreciate that self-regulation guidelines produced are a preliminary statement of the problem and remedies, and that further action for change can be expected.

Cross-gender coalition

The traumatisation of previously secure middle-level males in restructuring, and the experience of women being bullied by women (Hockley, 1998; Rylance, 2001; Thompson, 1998) has prompted a cross-gender sharing of concerns about unreasonable behaviours. Corporate directors and managers (mostly male), who have orchestrated conditions in which predominantly men, and some women, have treated both genders callously in restructuring, are also those holding the glass ceiling in place. In addition to men, women who display traditional masculine behaviours, and are complicit with the exercise of male power through bullying, may also help maintain the glass ceiling.

A lineage of action by women has been effective in establishing codes of conduct and refocusing the law, progressively, to address violence stemming predominantly from traditional masculine behaviours – through domestic violence, sexual harassment, discrimination and stalking. Most recently, this lineage manifested itself in QWWS's leadership of a cross-gender coalition in the development of industry self-regulation guidelines. The cross-gender sharing of concerns driving DBW reminds us that equal opportunity and harassment legislation addresses specific types of bullying that are residuals in the 'glass ceiling'. These concerns also alert us to the relevance of pursuing a wider notion of economic bullying.

Women bullies

The historical lineage of women adept at exercising power on a par with men – women warriors, Margaret Thatcher, and now Zena and Buffy the Vampire Slayer – suggests we should not be surprised that women might be able to bully like men. Indeed, some may have little option in many male-dominated workplaces other than to adorn themselves in male toughness to climb the corporate ladder. Recent research into incidences of women bullying women in predominantly female occupations suggests levels of bullying similar to those perpetrated by men (Hockley, 1998; McCarthy et al, 1995; Rylance, 1999; Thompson, 1998).

Suggestions that women could be bullies may stimulate moral panic, perhaps a reaction to perceived loss of virtue amongst women who appear to adopt traditional masculine behaviours. Recent literature certainly celebrates women's less confrontational, more consensual styles (Mapstone, 1998: 235). However positive, these attributions could be located in a lineage of virtuous constructions, for example, God's police, Florence Nightingale, and of excellence in domestic caring and secretarial support. Unfortunately, these stereotypes carry the stigma of weaker domesticism, and act to cap women's upward mobility in male-dominated workplaces where toughness is routinely rewarded. Interestingly, Mapstone reports women interviewees stressed their command capacities to her, seemingly taking their caring for granted, in contrast to male interviewees' new-age emphasis on concern for feelings (1998: 234).

We should be cautious about recent claims in the media that women are bullying more or are more adept at it. In addressing the first claim of women bullying more frequently than formerly, more diffuse workplace behaviours are now named 'bullying' with the increasing dominance of DBW. In addition, as women (very slowly) become more visible in supervisory and management positions, it becomes easier for them to be categorised as perpetrators.

In addressing the second claim, that women may be more adept at bullying than men, commonly held views that women's style of bullying is more domestic, bitchy, or ridiculing may well be a myth according to

Mapstone (1998: 251). Indeed, the stereotyping of women with a domestic mode of bullying may well reflect their lack of representation in positions of power, which more or less legitimates traditional male styles of bullying. Mapstone suggests that the very fact a women boss's behaviour does not fit traditional female stereotypes, for example, of listening, caring, nurturing and showing sensitivity, leaves her open to being labelled authoritarian, a bitch, inhuman or worse (1998: 251–2). In the maturing of soft-power and accompanying soft-violence in contemporary politics and organisation, these stereotypes could be applied to the argument that women could out-bully men in the soft-style. Soft-power is defined as 'the new medium by which influence is transmitted and wealth accumulated. Soft-power is about culture, values, entertainment, media image, financial flows, community reconciliation, technology and the Internet' (Kelly, 1999: 8). This less overt, more seductive exercise of power could also be seen to have its adjunct in soft-violence, as a subtler, more enmeshing and tacitly accepted coercion.

From a narrow perspective, new work teams that value more feminised interactions, including caring, networking and consensual problem-solving styles, could well be arenas in which women are more adept at bullying in the soft-style. To attribute significance to that possibility, however, is to overlook some key considerations. These include: the rhetorical nature of the discourse of the new work teams; their less than widespread operation in practice; the dominant male politics and controls within which these teams operate; and the negative stereotyping of the soft-style, which makes it difficult for women to advance in the corporate hierarchy.

In summary, DBW gives licence to speak of women as bullies and to dwell upon women as workplace bullies in male-dominated workplaces. This could, however, be triply victimising. Firstly, in relegating women to less powerful roles, secondly in attributing an emotionally manipulative style of bullying to them, and thirdly, in labelling them as better bullies than men.

Capacities for cruelty

A brief sketch of several predispositions of the perpetrator's desire, which are implicit in DBW, is provided in this section. Firstly, ways cruelty can heighten intensities of experiences, including pleasures in the exercise of power, are illustrated in Sade (1968). Perverse pleasures arising from territorial conquest, rape and killing in ethnic cleansing could be regarded as feudal precursors of the more sanitised excitations experienced by those successful in mean business, even in the interests of achieving national economic goals. Traumas of abrupt mass displacement and downscaling of life prospects are common to both, notwithstanding perpetrators' claims that the majority will be better off.

Furthermore, experiments by Zimbardo and by Milgram provide insights into ways 'normal', socially compliant persons can relay violence in acting out socially accepted roles. Milgram's experiment demonstrated a high level of compliance with authorisation of electric shocks to subjects. Indeed, an interpretation of the findings suggests that those more likely to initiate electric shocks were those more likely to comply with normal authority and social role expectations in everyday life (Gottfredson and Hirschi, 1993). Furthermore, Zimbardo's experiment illustrated that 'normal' college students could quickly turn into brutal prison guards. Notably, professional behaviours in the Holocaust stand as a fully developed precursor to those in Milgram's experiments. Findings in these experiments suggests the desire to comply socially has the potential to short circuit through soft-power, soft-violence and soft-fascism in the pressures of contemporary workplaces.

A more ingrained male predisposition to bullying behaviours can be found in the perspective that males carry a genetic evolutionary 'hard wiring' to express violence (Gatens and Pearson, 1999). Studies of the behaviour of chimpanzees identify evolutionary precursors of human corporate 'territorial games' (Simmons, 1998). While the rise of civil society is notable for the development of codes to restrain expressions of residual evolutionary dispositions to violence, a question of social complicity in preserving genetic pre-conditions for violence arises, given the potential for genetic engineering. For example, how many would favour elimination of the potential for violence and abuse in humans through genetic engineering? Would the product be non-human? Could collapse of the species be threatened by the elimination of the potential for 'good' violence, akin to that of immune reactions, as Baudrillard (1993) suggests? And, would courts accept 'don't blame me, blame my genes' arguments?

From Milgram and Zimbardo, and from the post-structuralists, we learn that violence is more evenly distributed in the human condition, with 'normal' people and social roles containing an inherent potential to transmit violence. These insights help deconstruct the bully–victim binary and assignments of 'good' and 'bad' implicit in DBW. They highlight the need for wider socio-economic, political and legal interventions to address the problem.

Victim-identity

The following discussion outlines ways in which desire might be invested in victim-identity, with both empowering and involuting effects. The discussion risks offending the integrity and dignity of victims, and I proceed with care in the interests of identifying moments in DBW that promise empowerment, yet continue the cycle of victimisation.

For those suffering distress in the pressures of contemporary workplaces, entering DBW is empowering, in that it helps make sense of one's life-world, and opens access to therapeutic interventions. A common refrain amongst victims entering the discourse is, 'At last I know what's been happening to me', accompanied by expression of relief, and a realisation that they are not alone in the world. For many, this affirmation is given reality through sharing stories with others.

A Foucauldian perspective helps us to see both liberating and entrapping moments in victim-identity. Those who adopt DBW's victim-identity open themselves to therapeutic interventions, by counsellors, psychiatrists, employee assistance providers, conflict-resolvers, interpersonal skills trainers, rehabilitators, trade unions and action groups. Other discourses may also be telescoped into victim-identity in a mutually empowering manner, including those of self-development (for example, coping and assertion), self-regulation, self-management, enterprise, and employee, human and legal rights. Characteristically, the development of a person's identity within DBW involves their learning to confess feelings in the language of the discourse.

Explanations as to why a person might enter positions of powerlessness and humiliation are also provided by theories of masochism. For example, mutually intensifying relations of pleasure and pain are illustrated by Sade (1968). In addition, Deleuze's (1991) commentary on Sacher Masoch's *Venus in Furs* explains how the masochist's control in choosing to enter a relationship in which the coldness and cruelty of the other party stimulates a perverse interplay of feelings between pain and self-confirmation. Implications for the professional–bully–victim triangle are that relations with cold and cruel others may carry their own peculiar satisfactions. Adoption of identities in the triangle may also be enterprising, as a strategy for survival and accumulation in a postmodern world.

The limits of victim-identity may be found in entrapment, where satisfactions of self-affirmation constrain 'becoming-healthy'. The 'unhealthy' limits of victim-identity may be modelled as a 'deadly practice of self' using a Deleuzian metaphor of the anorexic's illness. Therein, satisfactions in the anorexic's emaciation lie in the affirmation of desired bodily image: 'So the sicker people said I looked, the happier I was'

(Buchanan, 1997: 75). The inherent danger of this self-becoming is that 'far from accelerating becoming, what he or she actually does is deform it' (Buchanan, 1997: 87). In parallel terms, the limits of victimhood within DBW are also in the erasure of self in enduring stress breakdown and post-traumatic stress disorder (PTSD).

Soft-violence

The politics of soft-power in the Third Way advocated by Blair and Clinton also diffused into a softer face of power in Australia in politics, economy and organisation in the late 1990s. The discussion in this section explores ways soft-power might carry and legitimate soft-violence in which significant proportions of the populace are complicit. In addition, DBW is modelled as an exercise in soft-power, and the ways in which it could transmit 'ethical violence' are considered. Here ethical violence is regarded as violence stemming from soft-power policy-making, which legitimates the exercise of violence as a lesser evil, in the interests of the greater goods of market survival, consumption and accumulation.

The complicity of significant proportions of the populace in flows of soft-power through their desiring in these assemblages is notable: 'Soft-power encapsulates the mood and content of the 1990s' (Kelly, 1999: 8). Soft-power circulates through fears of falling, the desire to survive and consume, and infotainment.

> It is closely tied to the rise of the information age, the decline of national sovereignty, the loss of governmental influence, community disorientation at the pace of change, disillusionment with politics, the destruction of the barriers between news, politics and entertainment, and the phenomenon of 90s American triumphalism, whose real dynamic is creativity and innovation. (Kelly, 1999: 8)

The softer power of the Third Way is in its transcendence of political divisions, in a politics of affirmation driven by the complicity of a massified, postmodernised middle class. The information society provides capillaries, by which power is diffused and refracted through individuals as nodes throughout society. Softer violence manifests as every person becomes a Judge Judy, jury and punisher, bully and victim, calculator of lesser evils and greater goods, complicit in a vast interactive informational game of overcoming threats to market survival and to consumption.

The violence carried in the Kantian categorical imperative of 'do unto others as you would they do unto you' and into the utilitarian ethic of the 'greatest good for the greatest number', is now inverted through soft-power into risk management of futures in an ethically imperialist way, as 'do unto others *before* they do it to you'. The exercise of ethical imperialism can thus be seen as an essential moment in soft-power. In discussing violence in the interest of moral good, we should also be mindful that Eichmann invoked Kant, in stating his duty to follow Hitler's moral law, in his defence (Copjec, 1996: xvii).

Modelling DBW as a soft-power assemblage reveals limits at which it smoothes the transmission of soft-violence, including ethical imperialism, as not 'unreasonable' behaviours. At these limits, DBW can absolve us of responsibility for our desiring and the multiplicity of violences produced, by enabling the projective location of evil in the perpetrator–other. Beyond the limits of DBW we may discern conditions in which we are complicit, unknowingly guilty and responsible.

Market religiosity and sacrificial violence

According the market the status of a quasi-transcendental all-determining force in everyday life (Cox, 1999), places it in a realm beyond the responsibility of any person. Given widespread investment of desire in the market in the pursuit of survival and symbolic goods, there is a high potential for violence to flow from reactions to market gyrations in conditions of deregulation.

Within global market religiosity, DBW operates as a morality tale of fall and redemption. The professional–bully–victim trinity casts the victim as a casualty of a devil–perpetrator from the dark side of organisation. Their fall is a slow death, through stress, stress-breakdown, post-traumatic stress disorder, expulsion from work, and thoughts of suicide (Leymann, 1996). The victim's encounter with the professional offers redemption, normalisation of the pain in a wider life-world schema, and a pathway to resume 'normal' functioning.

A danger arises that each position within the professional–bully–victim trinity can be scapegoated as a devil–perpetrator, through a projecting out of sinfulness or violent feelings from one position onto the other. Realisation that one can be both bully and victim at any point in the professional–bully–victim trinity adds more subtle dimensions to questions of responsibility.

New tribal formations emerge as a reaction to uncertainty within market religiosity, and are functional in the pursuit of survival and accumulation. In these conditions, sacrificial mentality (Bataille, 1991) assumes new relevance, and is enacted through a multiplicity of sacrifices at the level of the individual and the organisation, including self-sacrifice.

Conditions for sacrifice were set by policy orientations of economic rationalism that became predominant in the 1990s, arguably fusing market religiosity, neo-classical economics and Darwinism. These policies routinely sacrifice life prospects of the poor. At the level of the organisation, employees' job tenures are commonly sacrificed in the interests of better market futures. The enterprising self is complicit in a multiplicity of little sacrifices, enmeshed in wider organisational and societal sacrifices in the trade of pleasure and pain. For example, participation at work in these conditions means taking one's share of pain in longer working hours and eroding pay and conditions. Yet many affirm the need for self-sacrifice at work, and trade off pain in constructing work as a site for survival and pleasure, through opportunities for interaction and consumption.

In the enterprising self we may discern lineages of self-sacrifice that runs deep in Western thought, in its heroic and Christian strands. Practices of self-sacrifice, through accepting pain and inflicting pain on others in the interests of survival and pleasure seem normalised at several levels in our life-worlds, including within politics (within soft-power); the economy (restructuring for better futures); workplaces (work intensification); interpersonal relations (your pain is my gain); and leisure (the highs and the limping in jogging, aerobics, gym).

Conclusion: Responsibility at the Limits of the Discourse Bullying-at-Work

Understanding ways that meanings are attributed to experiences of bullying in terms of *DBW* as a syndrome alerts us to the multiplicity of desires, identities and complicities at work. Mapping these relations helps us discern limits of the discourse beyond which victimisation can be compounded.

Awareness of these limits suggests responsibility for further change, given the risks of retribution and costs to persons speaking out about bullying, confronting their perpetrators, and taking action in tribunals or courts. Notwithstanding the release of guidelines in Queensland, we may reasonably conclude that efficient, safe access to remedies remains unavailable for most employees. The stresses, costs and benefits of action, through a maze of options of uncertain duration and outcome, remain unclear. The risk remains high of an individual being left worse off after taking action within the terms of the industry self-regulation guidelines. In these conditions, the introduction of enforceable compliance standards by the Division of Workplace Health and Safety (Qld) would be a positive exercise of political and professional responsibility.

The contours of meaning in DBW are continually evolving. Localised shared, lived experiences of unreasonable behaviours causing distress often escape the discourse and expose its limits. Responsibilities in civil, social democratic society encompass the need for 'good' people and victims not to remain silent, and to speak out about victimisation. At the level of the organisation, we need to open more channels through which distress can be given a voice and unreasonable behaviours challenged. Responsible managers can institute safeguards, such as protection from retribution and unfair dismissal. These can exist as part of developing cultures in which speaking out about distress is the norm. This would also be best practice in people skills and the management of diversity.

At the political level the development of DBW as a syndrome, and of industry self-regulation guidelines, are consequences of activism by responsible persons. The need remains, however, for ongoing political, social, economic and legal change to address structures, processes and ways of thinking that normalise bullying. Indeed, activism lies the other side of *No Exit* in the professional–bully–victim triangle, and for some may be the best therapy. Given the normalisation of soft-violence and widespread social compliance with 'reasonable behaviour' as a lesser 'evil' in the interests of greater socio-economic 'good', the need for vigilance remains high in the politics of soft-power.

A more balanced ecology of violence might recognise the diffusion of 'good' and 'evil' within every individual and social group, and self-sacrifice or self-bullying enabling structural and processual violences. Beyond DBW there is sense in dealing with the problem 'at home', at all points in the professional–bully–victim triangle, before embarking on projective resolutions.

Diffusion of responsibility to all points in the professional–bully–victim triangle is consistent with the devolution of social, political and organisational responsibilities in the politics of the Third Way. In a positive postmodern sense, this diffusion of responsibility opens multiple positions from which to address bullying behaviours, *if* all participants in the professional–bully–victim triangle are informed and accountable. Under these conditions, mapping dispositions of desire and complicity at all points helps develop more comprehensive understandings of the complexities of responsibility, and of individual duties and obligations.

A social postmodern coalition approach, across gender, cultural, socio-economic and generational divides, addressing responsibility for bullying that contributes to a range of contemporary social problems, offers good prospects for future action. Identifying the relations of desire, complicity and responsibility in professional–bully–victim triangles that contribute to problems such as youth suicide, deteriorating wealth distribution, unemployment, urban un-liveability, ageism, the glass-ceiling and racism, do seem worthwhile ways of proceeding.

References

Adams, A (1992) *Bullying at Work: How to Confront and Overcome It*. London: Virago.

Bataille, G (1991) *The Accursed Share*. New York: Zone Books.

Baudrillard, J (1993) *The Transparency of Evil: Essays on Extreme Phenomena*. London: Verso.

Buchanan, I (1997) 'The Problem of the Body, or What Can the Body Do?' 3(1) *Body and Society* 73–91.

Copjec, J (ed) (1996) *Radical Evil*. London: Verso.

Cox, H (1999) 'When Mammon is God', *Australian Financial Review*, 1 April, p 30.

Deleuze, G (1991) *Coldness and Cruelty in Masochism*. New York: Zone.

Division of Workplace Health and Safety (1998) *Workplace Bullying: An Employer's Guide*. Brisbane: Department of Employment, Training and Industrial Relations.

Ehrenreich, B (1990) *Fear of Falling: The Inner Life of the Middle Class*. New York: Harper Perennial.

Fillingham, L (1993) *Foucault for Beginners*. New York: Writers & Readers.

Gatens, M and Pearson, C (1999) 'Seeking to Soothe the Savage Beasts that are Men', *Australian Financial Review*, 5 March, p 8.

Gottfredson, M and Hirschi, T (1993) 'A Control Theory Interpretation of Psychological Research on Aggression', in R Felson, and J Tedeschi (eds), *Aggression and Violence: Social Interactionist Perspectives*. Washington, DC: American Psychological Association.

Hockley, C (1998) 'The Cost of Silence: Women Bullying Women', in P McCarthy, M Sheehan, S Wilkie and W Wilkie (eds), *Bullying: Causes, Costs, and Cures*. Brisbane: BBA.

Kelly, P (1999) 'Trivial New World' *The Australian, Review of Books*, 14 April, pp 7–8.

Leymann, H (1996) 'The Content and Development of Mobbing at Work' 5(2) *European Journal of Work and Organisational Psychology* 165–84.

McCarthy, P, Sheehan, M and Kearns, D (1995) *Managerial Styles and Their Effects on Employees' Health and Well-Being in Organisations Undergoing Restructuring*. Brisbane: School of Organisational Behaviour and Human Resource Management, Griffith University.

Mapstone, E (1998) *War of Words: Men and Women Arguing*. London: Chatto & Windus.

Milgram, S (1974) *Obedience to Authority: An Experimental View*. London: Tavistock.

Nicarthy, G, Gottleib, N and Goffman, S (1993) *You Don't Have to Take It! A Women's Guide to Confronting Emotional Abuse at Work*. Washington, DC: Seal Press.

Rylance, J (1999) 'Incongruent Behaviours and the Helping Professions'. Conference paper presented at the Responding to Professional Abuse Conference, University of Queensland, Brisbane, 2–3 July.

Sade, Marquis de (1968) *Juliette* (tr Austryn Warinhouse). New York: Grove.

Showalter, E (1997) *Hystories: Hysterical Epidemics and Modern Culture*. New York: Columbia University Press.

Simmons, A (1998) *Territorial Games: Understanding and Ending Turf Wars at Work*. New York: AMACOM.

Thompson, C (1998) *Workplace Bullying Project*. Adelaide: Working Women's Centre of SA, WorkCover and SA Health Commission Health Promotion Unit.

Zimbardo, P (1988) *Psychology and Life* (12th edn). New York: HarperCollins.

Chapter 10

Health and Safety Guidelines to Address Bullying at Work

Cath Rafferty

The Context of Workplace Bullying in the 1990s

Complaints of workplace bullying reached critical mass during the 1990s and started receiving serious attention when legal claims began to succeed in the civil courts. Prior to this period, workplace bullying was seen to fit within the context of 'personality conflict' rather than being an industrial issue in its own right, and consequently was considered to be an insoluble problem, unsuitable for normal dispute-settling procedures. There were a number of factors that made workplace bullying a 1990s' phenomenon:

- In earlier times people were able to leave a job if they were bullied. With a shrinking job market, resignation is not a realistic option, which leads to increasing complaints of this type of behaviour.
- With the introduction of anti-discrimination legislation, people are becoming more aware of their rights and believe that this legislation covers all forms of harassment and discrimination, whereas it is very specific.
- The introduction of unfair dismissal provisions into the *Workplace Relations Act* 1996 (Cth) and the industrial relations regimes of some States have convinced managers and employers that they cannot sack an employee without good reason. Bullying is sometimes used as a way of harassing an employee into resigning from his or her job.
- The 1990s' workforce is very highly educated, due to increased school retention rates in the 1980s and increasing levels of adult training. The changing profile of the workforce carries with it new expectations of a less authoritarian and a more consultative, responsive and inclusive workplace culture for employees and employer.

> There appears to be a lag between expectations and current workplace culture, resulting in a higher level of dissatisfaction with bullying behaviour than in previous decades.

Bullying has been used as a management tool. The practice of restructuring and downsizing can magnify power imbalances and job insecurities, and encourage an atmosphere of corporate bullying. Changes of management or ownership in business can also lead to the use of bullying tactics to sweep out existing staff.

Same sex environments can engender a culture of bullying. For example, all-male manufacturing workshops may condone bullying practices and all-female nursing homes may use bullying as part of the pecking order. Bullying has a psychological profile, which has identified the typical bully as extroverted, and goal- and achievement-oriented rather than rules- or process-oriented. A typical victim has been identified as a strong but introverted personality with concern for following rules and processes, and 'getting things right' rather than 'getting things done'.

Individuals who bully use power attributed to status or position, for example, their number of years with a company, or personal power based on their belief that they are always right, or referred power based on people they know in authority. These people can single out a person with less power to befriend and help, and then move on, leaving them isolated. Victims may be anyone. We all have the capacity to be the bully or the target of a bully. Victims do not necessarily have low self-esteem, or display a non-assertive or victim attitude.

In our experience victims may come from all walks of life, from kitchen hands to professionals. Anyone can find themselves in situations they find impossible to cope with. Consequently, human resource managers need to be aware that anyone can fall into the role of bully or victim, given the right circumstances.

The Queensland Experience: Developing Workplace Bullying Guidelines

Rationale for developing guidelines

Over a four-year period, complaints to the Queensland Working Women's Service (QWWS) rose from 10% of all queries in 1995 and 1996 to 27% of all queries in 1997 and 1998. This represents almost 1000 complaints from clients of workplace bullying in one year alone, which indicates the level of dysfunctional workplaces in Queensland and the number of very unhappy workers putting pressure on medical and legal services. In a recent Morgan & Banks survey, 14.8% of employers in Queensland considered bullying at work was on the increase and that it was a significant workplace problem. Recent figures quoted by the Queensland academic Paul McCarthy from the Beyond Bullying Association in the *Bulletin* estimate that 350,000 people in Australia currently experience systematic bullying in the workplace, with costs of up to $3 billion a year in sick leave, absenteeism, staff turnover, low productivity, legal action, workers' compensation and social security.

The process of establishing guidelines

From 1996, voluntary agencies, such as the QWWS, the Beyond Bullying Association, raised the issue of workplace bullying in the public domain:

- QWWS developed publications and a counselling service on how to handle workplace bullying;
- it took the leading role in organising forums in Brisbane in 1996, 1997, 1998 and 1999;
- it established a network of key stakeholders across employers, unions, lawyers, the Beyond Bullying Association and the government to develop an industry code of conduct on workplace bullying;
- it negotiated with the Division of Workplace Health and Safety to develop guidelines for employers and workers on workplace bullying;
- QWWS chaired the advisory committee that worked on the project in 1998; and
- QWWS organised the forums in November 1998 and February 1999 at which Minister Paul Braddy launched the guidelines.

The guidelines are the first initiative for any government in Australia in naming and tackling the issue of workplace bullying. QWWS views these guidelines as the first step towards reducing the incidence of workplace bullying. They are not prescriptive but they do provide a formal recognition of the issue by government and a best practice model for employers. The strength of the guidelines is the model they provide for an overall policy that targets all forms of inappropriate behaviour, from abusive language and practical jokes to sexual harassment and discrimination. In this way, the guidelines are comprehensive and inclusive of both genders and all ages.

The Content of the Guidelines

Definition of workplace bullying

Workplace bullying is a term that covers a multitude of behaviours. Basically it is a broad description covering both overt harassment, such as verbal abuse, hostility, rages, tirades, and covert harassment such as sabotage, isolation and undermining an individual's position. The common ground is that a person has been treated less favourably and has suffered an injury due to behaviour that is beyond normal disciplinary action or appropriate workplace interaction. Bullying behaviour can occur at any level within an organisation, both between co-workers or within a vertical power relationship (such as between manager and owner or supervisor and employee). A useful definition used in *Workplace Bullying: An Employer's Guide* is 'the repeated less favourable treatment of a person by another or others in the workplace, which may be considered unreasonable and inappropriate workplace practice'. It includes behaviour that intimidates, offends, degrades or humiliates a worker, possibly in front of co-workers, clients or customers. Overt bullying behaviour may include:

- shouting and swearing repeatedly at staff in public or in private;
- rages, particularly over trivial matters;
- humiliating staff in public;
- insults and name-calling;
- persistent criticism.

Covert bullying behaviour may include:

- deliberately sabotaging or impeding work performance;
- refusing to delegate;
- constantly changing targets or work guidelines;
- withholding information or supplying incorrect information;
- setting people up to fail through impossible deadlines for an increased workload.

Bullying behaviours between co-workers include:

- teasing;
- practical jokes;
- isolating co-workers;
- criticising co-workers.

Workplace Bullying Scenarios

Overt bullying: work rage

Client X was employed by a medium-sized legal firm. During the first year of employment, the client experienced the following behaviours from the employer, who was a partner in the firm:

- irrational outbursts regarding trivial matters, such as using a paper clip instead of a staple;

- use of abusive and foul language intended to humiliate and degrade staff personally and professionally – in person, over the phone and on the Dictaphone;
- unreasonable demands regarding workload;
- literally throwing things, such as files, tapes, mail and messages at staff, causing them to work in an atmosphere of constant stress and anxiety;
- irrational behaviour, making it impossible to discuss or resolve any issue. In fact, staff were generally terrified of the employer and fearful of reactions to complaints.

Covert bullying: career sabotage

Client Y was employed as an account director of a regional office by a national marketing firm. The client was performing well, achieving good outcomes, particularly on a major national account, until a new interstate senior executive arrived to take over the branch. Over the following months, it became clear that the new executive did not want Client Y on the team. The following tactics were documented by the client:

- the client's major account was taken over by the new executive;
- promised support staff were shifted to other areas;
- a change of title effectively demoted the client;
- a redesign of office layout isolated the client from other senior staff;
- the client was excluded from team meetings;
- the client was abused about work performance in front of peers;
- extra work demands were made on the client that were not made on work colleagues;
- the client was vulnerable to being made redundant when the company downsized.

These two scenarios illustrate the widely differing experiences of workplace bullying. The first scenario is an example of overt bullying behaviour due to irrational treatment or work rage. The second scenario is an example of covert bullying, which is based on a strategy of sabotage, silence and isolation. In both cases gender may not be an issue. Victim and perpetrator may be either male or female. The impact on the individual and the organisation will be equally devastating.

Agencies such as QWWS advise clients every day about workplace behaviour that reflects the two scenarios above and all the varieties in between. We witness the story of personal toll and demoralisation daily. Whatever the experience, the outcome is the same, with grown people reduced to quivering wrecks, shadows of their former selves, with their health, confidence and self-esteem seriously affected.

The Impact on the Employee and Organisation

The impacts on the employee can range from:

- time off work due to stress, depression or a nervous disorder;
- enforced resignation, redundancy or termination of employment;
- medical or legal costs that may result from the injury.

The impacts on the workplace can include:

- a dysfunctional environment resulting in low productivity and poor morale;
- adverse publicity, poor public image, and becoming known as a difficult workplace;
- costs associated with failure to meet legislative provisions, WorkCover claims, civil action, criminal action or personal injuries claims.

Employers' Obligations to Prevent Bullying in the Workplace

The rationale for employers to prevent workplace bullying is dictated by both good management and legal obligations. The common law imposes general obligations on employers, relevant to bullying. An employer is under a duty of care to protect workers from workplace bullying. This duty exists:

- in tort, as negligence (failure to provide a safe workplace) and defamation;
- as an implied term in the employment contract, that the employer would not, without reasonable cause, destroy or seriously damage the relationship of trust and confidence between employer and worker.

Employers who do not take suitable precautions to protect workers from workplace bullying may be liable for any physical or psychological injury suffered by the victim. Recent cases are setting precedents for workplace bullying to be dealt with under personal injury claims with some significant compensation payments.

Vicarious liability

Liability is a legal term that means an individual is personally responsible for his or her own unlawful acts. In the workplace employers can be held liable for unlawful acts committed by their employees in the course of their work. This principle is known as vicarious liability.

Vicarious liability can be reduced or avoided altogether if the employer can show that they took all reasonable steps to prevent the sexual harassment or discrimination occurring. This means that employers are required to implement precautions to minimise the risk of unlawful behaviour occurring in the workplace. Employers must not only introduce policies but must also demonstrate that they have actively disseminated and implemented these policies throughout the workplace. Whilst there is no legislation that specifically prevents bullying, certain types of bullying (such as assault, sexual harassment and discrimination) are against the law. Individuals suffering the effects of serious bullying (such as constructive dismissal, unfair dismissal, illness and incapacity to work) can have redress through existing legislation. Some of the legal and legislative frameworks in place apply nationally, and some of these are reinforced by State laws. Generally, these laws are found under the headings of:

- workplace health and safety or occupational health and safety;
- anti-discrimination
- human rights and equal opportunity
- workplace relations
- industrial relations
- WorkCover or ComCare
- public ethics or public service.

Health and safety legislation

Employers have an obligation to ensure the health and safety of their workers under both the *Workplace Health and Safety Act* 1995 (Qld) and the *Occupational Health and Safety (Commonwealth Employment) Act* 1991 (Cth). Health and safety is ensured when people are free from injury or illness, or death, caused by any workplace, workplace activity or specified high risk plant, or the risk of death, injury or illness (*Workplace Health and Safety Act* 1995 (Qld) s 22). Workplace health and safety can generally be managed by (s 22):

- identifying hazards;
- assessing the risks that may result because of the hazards;
- deciding on control measures to prevent or minimise the level of risks;
- implementing control measures;
- and monitoring and reviewing the effectiveness of the measures.

Employers may be held vicariously liable for the actions of their employees, or for failure to take appropriate action to resolve a situation. In certain circumstances verbal abuse, intimidation and humiliation may be viewed as occupational violence.

Anti-discrimination and harassment legislation

Where bullying involves acts of discrimination or sexual harassment, a complaint may be lodged under the *Anti-Discrimination Act* 1991 (Qld), the *Sex Discrimination Act* 1984 (Cth), the *Disability Discrimination Act* 1992 (Cth), the *Racial Discrimination Act* 1975 (Cth) or the *Human Rights and Equal Opportunity Commission Act* 1986 (Cth). Sexual harassment is any form of unwelcome attention of a sexual nature, which is humiliating, intimidating or offensive. Discrimination occurs when someone is treated less favourably due to:

- sex;
- race;
- age;
- impairment;
- pregnancy;
- parental status;
- marital status;
- religion;
- political belief or activity;
- trade union activity;
- lawful sexual activity;
- or association with a person having any of the above-mentioned attributes.

Under the above legislation, both the harasser and the employer may be held vicariously liable for the action of employees who contravene the Act, unless they can demonstrate they have taken all reasonable steps to prevent the acts from occurring.

Industrial relations legislation

Where a worker is dismissed or forced to resign as a result of workplace bullying, the worker may be entitled to make a claim under the unfair dismissal provisions of the *Industrial Relations Act* 1999 (Qld) or the *Workplace Relations Act* 1996 (Cth). Most industrial awards contain grievance procedures, which can be used in disputes involving workplace bullying.

Where a dispute involving workplace bullying is between an employer and a worker (as opposed to one between co-workers), a person can lodge a Notice of Industrial Dispute with the Industrial Relations Commission.

Workers' compensation

A worker may submit a claim for workers' compensation under the *WorkCover Queensland Act* 1996 (Qld) if workplace bullying has contributed to a workplace injury. A diagnosable psychological or psychiatric condition may also be considered for workers' compensation if it is work related. A worker is an individual who performs a work under a contract of service.

A worker may have a stress claim if the injury has arisen out of, or in the course of, employment if the employment is a significant contributing factor causing the injury. However, 'injury' does not include a psychiatric or psychological disorder that has arisen out of, or in the course of:

- reasonable management action taken in a reasonable way by the employer in connection with the worker's employment;
- the worker's expectation or perception of reasonable management action being taken against the worker;
- action by WorkCover or a self-insurer in connection with the worker's application for compensation.

Public sector ethics

In Queensland the *Public Sector Ethics Act* 1994 (Qld) and federally the *Public Service Act* 1999 (Cth) provide guides to the development of a Code of Conduct and also provide that disciplinary action can be taken for contravention of the Code of Conduct. The *Public Sector Ethics Act* 1994 provides for obligations concerning the treatment of members of the public and public officials by being honest and fair, and providing proper regard for their rights and obligations. The *Public Service Act* 1999 (Cth) provides for Australian Public Service employees to behave honestly and with integrity and also provides that they treat everyone with respect and courtesy, and without harassment.

Criminal code

Where bullying involves physical assault or the threat of assault, the incident becomes a police matter and is dealt with under the Queensland *Criminal Code*:

- aiding and abetting: s 7;
- assault: s 245;
- common assault: s 335;
- assault at work: s 346;
- assault occasioning bodily harm: s 339;
- grievous bodily harm: s 320.

Steps for Employers to Reduce Workplace Bullying

The employer can:

- **investigate the existence of bullying** through consultation with employees and union delegates, monitoring patterns of absenteeism, workers' compensation claims, exit interviews and even suggestion boxes;
- **develop a written policy** on workplace bullying that promotes respectful behaviour, which is fully supported by the employer and displayed throughout the workplace (the guidelines include an example of a model policy that can be adapted to individual businesses);
- **appoint a contact person** who may be an existing employee or an outside agent to provide confidential advice and assistance;
- **implement a procedure for handling complaints** about workplace bullying that includes both an informal resolution process between the complainant and the alleged bully and a formal complaints process covering a grievance procedure, an investigation and resolution process, an appeal mechanism, access to counselling and mediation;
- **inform and train** managers, supervisors, and existing and new workers about the policy to reduce bullying in the workplace;
- **review and evaluate the strategy** to ensure success and continued effectiveness.

Steps for Employees to Complain about Workplace Bullying

- **The employee can take comprehensive notes of all incidents,** times, dates, what was said, what was done, and who was there. Bullying behaviour can be almost impossible to prove to the satisfaction of your organisation. They will only see the positive, productive side of the alleged bully. Therefore a diary of events, recording incidents in detail, can be the basis for a formal or informal complaint and can be used in evidence in a court of law or a tribunal.
- **The employee can check for a relevant policy within the organisation.** There may be a procedure for raising the bullying issue within the company if it can link into existing policies on, for example, consultation, respectful behaviour, and treating staff as clients or customers. Some companies now have comprehensive policies covering the elimination of all forms of harassment, not only sexual harassment.
- **The employee can seek alternative avenues of support within the company.** This includes approaching supportive colleagues, re-

questing confidential advice from a manager or supervisor, finding out whether the company employs a health and safety officer, an equity or sexual harassment referral officer or an employee assistance officer. In addition, it is possible to use family members as a support network in approaching management.

- **The employee can seek assistance from a trade union,** if the employee is a member or is joining a union. The union plays a role in advocating for its members within the workplace.
- **The employee can report a psychological injury to a medical practitioner,** if the employee is obliged to take leave of absence due to stress, depression or sickness because of workplace bullying. In addition, it may be useful for the employee to fill out an incident report form at work, particularly if they are considering filing for workers' compensation.
- **The employee can submit a WorkCover claim.** This may be an option where bullying behaviour results in a psychological or physical injury that makes it impossible for the employee to continue at work. However, the claimant must be able to prove that work was a significant contributing factor to the injury, that the injury was not the result of normal disciplinary processes and that it passes the 'reasonable person' test. It should be noted that such claims can be lengthy and invasive about personal circumstances, for example, seeking proof in the form of witnesses of the incidents, and are often unsuccessful, causing the claimant greater distress.
- **The employee can report the incidents to the workplace health and safety inspector,** particularly where the bullying behaviour is causing a hazard in the workplace. Incidents of occupational violence or conflict between co-workers fall into this category. However, psychological injury through bullying does not usually meet the evidence requirements under the *Workplace Health and Safety Act* 1995 (Qld) or the *Occupational Health and Safety (Commonwealth Employment) Act* 1991 (Cth) and presents difficulties for inspectors to isolate as a health hazard.
- **The employee can make a claim under anti-discrimination legislation.** If the harassment is based on discrimination linked to the employee's sex, race, age, impairment, pregnancy, parental status, marital status, religion, political beliefs or activities, lawful sexual activity or association with a person having any of the abovementioned attributes, the employee may be eligible to submit a claim under the federal or State anti-discrimination legislation.
- **The employee can check for grievance procedures in the award, contract of employment or company policy covering the em-**

ployee. Awards are legally binding documents outlining work conditions and pay rates. Most awards contain a grievance procedure and this should be followed in an attempt to resolve the situation. Basically this means submitting a letter or statement of complaint to the supervisor or manager. Employees have the right to union representation at all stages of the procedure if they are members. If nothing is resolved inhouse, then a notification of dispute can be lodged with the Industrial Relations Commission.

- **The employee can seek the intervention of dispute resolution services** where mediation is required within the workplace. Where both parties are willing to take part in a mediation conference over workplace bullying behaviour, a dispute resolution service will supply a mediator at the work site.
- **The employee can check the ramifications of any action taken** either with the union, the relevant government agency or an agency such as QWWS. The injured party needs to feel both secure in making a complaint, and that the situation at work will not deteriorate as a result of the complaint. They may require some form of psychological support through counselling to give them the necessary confidence to handle the incidents or to resign and seek other employment.

As outlined above, there are no clear solutions or legal remedies for the victims of workplace bullying. However, the guidelines can provide a valuable tool when implemented for prevention, early detection and quick resolution of complaints.

Bibliography

Division of Workplace Health and Safety (1998) *Workplace Bullying: An Employer's Guide*. Brisbane: Department of Employment, Training and Industrial Relations.

Spry, M (1998) 'Workplace Harassment: What is It, and What Should the Law do about It?' 40(2) *Journal of Industrial Relations* 232–46.

Chapter 11

Bullying of Victims by Present Injustices in the System

Peter Gorman

Natural Justice

Over many years a procedure known as natural justice has evolved through the various arms of the law and the legal system. The rules and procedures of natural law are to be followed by any person or body charged with the duty of adjudicating on disputes or the rights of others, for example, a government department.

The chief rules are to act fairly, in good faith without bias, and in a judicial temper; to give each party the opportunity of adequately stating his or her case, and correcting or contradicting any relevant statement prejudicial to his or her case; and not to hear one side behind the back of the other. Individuals or systems, for example, a government department, must not be judges in their own cause, so that a judge must declare any interest he or she has in the subject matter of the dispute before him or her. A person must have notice of anything he or she is accused of. Relevant documents that are looked at by any tribunal or court should be disclosed to the parties interested. In short, not only should justice be done, but it should be seen to be done (Osborn, 1992: 217).

One can see, therefore, that it will not be too far in the future where people who are victims of bullying will be represented by lawyers in their cases so that they can be given the opportunity of adequately stating their own case and correcting or contradicting any relevant statement prejudicial to their case.

As a result of their experience, most victims of bullying I have come across do not have sufficient communication skills and confidence to prepare their own case adequately and act as their own advocate. To this end, legal aid should be provided, because individuals who are victims of bullying and who are suffering from a reactive depression, prolonged stress disorder or a stress and anxiety disorder, clearly cannot verbalise their cases for themselves.

In my experience it is rare for legal aid to be available, even in the worst of cases, to assist the victims so that they know their rights and the remedies available, and receive sound advice as to which direction they should follow. Legal aid has become a large bureaucracy in Queensland, which has failed since 1993 to raise the funding for the legal practitioners who work at legal aid scales to assist people in our community. The blame does not lie wholly at the door of the legal aid system: neither the States nor the federal government has funded areas of legal defence in which a great deal of difficulty is experienced by so many ordinary members of the public.

In the Morgan & Banks *Job Index* (1999), it was reported that the cost to Australians of bullying in the workplace was between three and four billion dollars per annum, with a suspected ripple effect of 20 billion dollars per annum. The *Job Index* stated that workplace bullies were on the rise. A significant number of employers (10.4%) believed that bullying at work was increasing. Industries where the perception of bullying was highest included tourism, with a very high rate of 20.7%, the health/medical/pharmaceutical industries with a rate of 15.5%, the legal sector with a rate of 14.5%, the government sector with a rate of 14.1%, and the media with a rate of 14%. Fewer employers in the electronics and engineering industries thought bullying was prevalent, with a rate of 4.3% and 4.6% respectively. More employers from large businesses (13%) thought bullying was increasing. Small business operators have less of a problem, with 10% of them saying bullying was on the rise, and medium-size businesses, with 8.6%, were the least concerned with the problem.

Clearly, early intervention by a discipline that is aware of rights and remedies will go a long way towards reducing the cost of bullying to the community. The comparatively small amount paid for legal aid could, with education and early intervention, reduce the overall bill.

Is There a Legal Remedy?

The first question, however, is about what kinds of workplace behaviour give rise to legal consequences. Workplace bullying may be expensive, but if the victim has no legal protection, then no amount of legal aid will assist.

The whole of Australia is covered by the *Workplace Relations Act* 1996 (Cth) s 52D. This Act has governed all federal industrial awards and all Australian workplace agreements and awards since 1 January 1997, and s 52D contains provisions for dispute (grievance) resolution. Victoria has transferred its industrial relations powers to the Commonwealth, so that the section applies throughout the State. The other States have their own legislation, which covers workplaces and employment issues not covered by the federal Act.

Queensland has dispute resolution provisions (*Industrial Relations Act* 1997 s 127), which are virtually identical to s 52D of the federal Act. What follows is a discussion of the Queensland position. However, it applies equally to the position under the federal Act, as the grievance procedure under the two sections is the same. Readers outside Queensland (other than in Victoria) should check their own State's legislation unless they are covered by a federal award or an Australian Workplace Agreement.

Grievance Procedures in Queensland

In each of the State awards since the early 1990s, and in each Queensland Workplace Agreement (QWA), there is a procedure set out to ensure grievance procedures are included. In the *Industrial Relations Act* 1999 (Qld), s 127 points out that an award must provide for a dispute resolution procedure. If a procedure is not included, Sch 2 to the *Industrial Relations Regulation* 2000 (Qld) would apply and a dispute resolution procedure would be included in any award and QWA.

One of the difficulties with these awards is that many people in authority, including employers, do not understand the reasons for grievance procedures, and therefore no protocols are set out to resolve disputes in their early stages.

Dispute Resolution Procedures

Section 127 (1) The commission must ensure an award contains a dispute resolution procedure.

(2) The form of the procedure is to be agreed on by the parties to the award.

(3) However, if the parties cannot agree, the commission must insert an appropriate proceeding in the award.

(4) Without limiting subsection (1), the procedure must include –

(a) procedures for consultation at the workplace; and
(b) procedures for the involvement of relevant organisations; and
(c) any other procedure prescribed under a regulation.

These grievance procedures have been introduced to Queensland awards since the early 1990s, and few people are aware of their existence. The

Queensland experience follows the setting up in England by the *Industrial Relations (Code of Practice) Order* 1972 (Statutory Instrument 1972 No 179), of a similar English procedure. Litigation in England has shown that these grievance procedures are of the utmost importance.

In the English case of *Gould Ltd v McConnell* [1995] IRLR 516, Justice Morison said, 'It is clear therefore that parliament considers that good industrial relations require employers to provide their employees with a method of dealing with grievances in a proper and timely fashion.'

Of course, this was also consistent with codes of practice. That being so, the industrial tribunal was entitled to conclude that there was an implied term in the contract of employment that the employers should reasonably and promptly provide a reasonable opportunity to their employees to obtain redress for any grievance they may have had. It was rightly conceded that a breach of this implied term would be a breach of contract.

Further, it seems that the right to obtain redress for a grievance is fundamental, since the working environment might well lead to employees experiencing difficulties for a variety of reasons, including the fact that authority and control is sometimes exercised by individuals insufficiently experienced to exercise it wisely.

There is a provision in the *Industrial Relations Act* 1999 (Qld), which came into force on 1 July 1999, that where a QWA exists, a party to that agreement must not contravene the QWA (s 215). Indeed, the Act, which replaced the *Workplace Relations Act* 1997 (Qld), goes further; under s 219, a party to a QWA who suffers loss or damage because of a contravention of the QWA by the other party may recover the amount of the loss or damage in an Industrial Magistrate's Court. An individual must bring this action, similar to loss of wages, within six years after the date on which the cause of the action arose. One notes that in the *Industrial Relations Act* 1999 (Qld), the terminology refers to a QWA, whereas the *Workplace Relations Act* 1997 (Qld) referred to an award. Where there was an award earlier and a QWA comes into existence, then the QWA will cover the areas in question. Again these grievance procedures are quite complex and need to be looked at and followed quickly, but without legal aid there is little chance of any person bringing them to the notice of the victims.

The *Workplace Relations Act* 1996 (Cth), which has governed federal awards and Australian workplace agreements and awards since 1 January 1997, contains provisions for dispute (grievance) resolution. Section 52D of the federal Act sets out provisions very similar to the Queensland Act and incorporates the provisions to apply in Victoria.

Failure to Provide Early Intervention, Aid and Support Properly

In the *WorkCover Queensland Act* 1996, s 249(1) provides that workers must participate in rehabilitation as soon as is practicable after an injury has occurred. This makes the whole thing a nonsense, since most injured workers cannot afford rehabilitation off their own bat and therefore have to wait for WorkCover to process their claim.

Under s 161(2) of the Act, WorkCover has six months in which to make a decision. Should they fail to make a decision in that time, workers can apply to an Industrial Magistrate's Court for a determination of the matter. In my view, and in that of many others, this six-month period is far too long. Indeed, in the UK the period is one month. The Queensland State government made tentative promises earlier this year to reduce the period to three months, but so far that has not been implemented. Indeed, in Queensland workers could be further delayed if the processing of their claim takes almost six months and the claim is refused. Then there is a further period of internal review, during which time the victim presumably has no treatment, as it is not sanctioned by the processing of the claim in their favour.

As from 1 July 1999, the *Workcover Amendment Act* 1999 (Qld) reduced the effect of s 161(2) to a period of three months for WorkCover to consider the worker's application. Experience since that time has shown that this is not yet being complied with.

A number of lawyers and other individuals interested in the welfare of victims have had difficulty with the Internal Review Unit of WorkCover. This author knows of only one appeal succeeding, and that was by an employer against an employee receiving compensation for the injury received. When one looks at the aspects of natural justice, one can see that it is difficult to become a judge in one's own cause. This does nothing to help the injured victim.

The question of early intervention is raised again by s 238, which specifies that WorkCover must take steps to ensure an early return to duties. Of course, this cannot happen until the claim is processed, and time ticks quickly by. Psychiatrists and psychologists will be aware that a condition changes from *acute* to *chronic* after a period of between three and six months, thereby making it more difficult for people with depressions and anxiety disorders to recover quickly when they have to wait so long to receive proper treatment. Early treatment is essential and should be ensured, as the Act requires.

In the case of *Carrigan v Darwin City Council*, in a decision of von Doussa J on 20 March 1997 in the Industrial Relations Court of Australia, the judge found that the City Council's failure to implement rehabilitation procedures properly was in breach of the implied contract of employment and awarded an increase of compensation to the maximum for constructive dismissal. What von Doussa J said was similar to what the High Court in *McLean v Tedman* (1984) 155 CLR 306, which stated, 'that the duty to provide a safe system of work extends to maintaining and enforcing it'. It could not be used solely as window dressing.

Ramifications of Incorrectly Filled-in Pro formas

Difficulties can arise where claimants are required to fill in pro forma claim forms. In 1999, WorkCover introduced a new claim form, with the aim of reducing problems arising from the complexities of the system. It is too early to establish whether this form works better.

In the past I have been involved in a number of cases where the injured worker has applied for WorkCover and other benefits, only to be criticised for failing to tick every box and give a full explanation on the one short line of about five centimetres long provided in the form. The clerks who assist in supplying the victims with forms should, in my view, work together with the claimants to bring about a standardisation of what is filled in, rather than the victim having the indignity of being cross-examined in front of an industrial magistrate as to why this, that or the other was not put into the form, when it is obvious that the form is not big enough and has no provision for the proper answers to be included. Furthermore, victims are in no condition to analyse and weigh up the pros and cons properly or the ramifications of filling in the form incorrectly, when they are unfamiliar with these forms. This will make life extremely difficult for them at the Industrial Magistrates Court at some date in the future, by which time they will have had little or no intervention to cure the condition from which they are suffering and for which they are applying for workers' compensation. However, in late 1999 a much simpler pro forma was introduced, which should reduce the problems caused by the complexities of the previous system.

Failure to Advise of Alternative Financial Assistance

One of the difficulties that people face, and which is a present injustice in the system, is that when they apply for compensation or other benefits, usually through their spouse or partner, they are not told of the alternatives available to them. Union officials should be more proactive at this time, when a worker falls sick or is so ill they cannot continue working. It would prevent a great deal of unnecessary hardship for the victims and their families if they were aware of the following.

(a) Until the compensation is granted to them and paid, they can claim Social Security benefits in certain circumstances.
(b) In Queensland, if they are members of the public service, they may be able to receive 75% of their normal pay for a maximum period of two years, provided they belong to Queensland Super (Q-Super). One of the other superannuation companies that assists fire officers is much more beneficial. Union officials should therefore find out what financial benefits are due to individuals in this situation.

The answer, of course, is education. It is difficult to achieve with the regular shortages in government funding, but education will help to inform people of the various avenues open to them.

Lengthy Delays in Listing Matters before Industrial Magistrates

There is a gap in the legislation between anti-discrimination and industrial and workplace relations. As a result, people do not know that some industrial relations matters may go not only to the Industrial Relations Commission but also to the Industrial Magistrate, for example, if grievance procedures break down and are not resolved satisfactorily. Some matters may go to the anti-discrimination tribunals, but once the industrial relations matter is registered, it is held in abeyance until the determination of the anti-discrimination tribunal hearing.

There should be some way of joining the two together, perhaps through the matter of judicial appointments, whereby bullying in the workplace is acknowledged as often both an industrial matter and an anti-discrimination matter. Indeed, the need appears to be obvious when one looks at the definition of workplace bullying as 'the repeated less favourable treatment of a person by another or others in a workplace, which may be considered unreasonable and inappropriate workplace practice' (Division of Workplace Health and Safety, 1998). This was part of the Protocol put out in November 1998 by the Queensland Division of Workplace Health and Safety, after 12 months of consultations with various representatives, including myself.

Looking forward, one can only espouse the principles of the Beyond Bullying Association, that public awareness and education be increased so that early intervention can take place and cut down this drain on the economy.

References

Division of Workplace Health and Safety (1998) *Workplace Bullying: An Employer's Guide*. Brisbane: Department of Employment, Training and Industrial Relations.

Morgan & Banks (1999) *Job Index* (February–April). Melbourne: Morgan & Banks.

Osborn's Concise Law Dictionary (1992, 5th edn). London: Sweet & Maxwell.

Chapter 12

Eliminating Professional Abuse by Managers

Michael Sheehan

Setting the Scene

In *The Nature of Managerial Work*, Henry Mintzberg (1973) stated that the prime occupational hazard of the manager is superficiality, one of the by-products of time pressure. Since then, time pressure on leaders, managers, other professionals and employees has increased. Such pressure can lead to abuse, particularly in the name of getting the job done (Cooper, 1997). The issue of increasing pressure placed on managers today leads to potential problems for managers, employees and organisations alike.

One costly consequence of the relentless demands on managers' time is their subsequent propensity to adhere as closely as possible to the realm of facts and intellect, and to value only things that can be ordered, analysed, defined, dealt with, corralled and contained (Mintzberg, 1989; Peters, 1993). Friction or conflict between the parties involved only heightens this propensity. The likelihood of abuse by managers towards employees, as a result of the stresses placed on the managers to perform, needs to be acknowledged.

We need to ask ourselves: *are managers' actions in the modern workplace appropriate within our understanding of managers as professionals?* In posing this question, the terms 'management' and 'manager' are used interchangeably, as are 'profession', 'professionals' and 'professionalism'. If managers' actions are congruent with the way in which professionals are prescribed to act, then abuse by managers in the workplace is unprofessional – such abusive actions are incongruent with how professionals should act.

The under-development of people skills or 'soft skills' in managers dealing with organisational demands, including the rapidity, ambiguity and uncertainty of change, may contribute to the problem of abuse in the workplace. In suggesting a positive strategy for overcoming the problem, it is important to examine the concept of emotional intelligence. One way to help address the problem of managerial abuse may be to develop the emotional intelligence of managers.

Three aims are noted in exploring the concept of managerial professionalism. Given current conditions of organisational change and uncertainty, the first is to explore whether or not managers are in fact professionals. The second is to present evidence suggesting that within the definition of managers and within that of professionals, some managers are not professional. The third is to present a possible solution as to how to redress the problem of abuse by these non-professional managers in the workplace. This will help restore the status of managers as professionals and contribute to more productive and efficient organisations by seeking to minimise the problem of abuse by managers.

What Shapes a Manager?

Understanding what shapes a manager is a difficult task. Despite many years of management research, there is a lack of a coherent knowledge base to guide our understanding (Peters and Smith, 1998). Nonetheless, some common themes emerge from the literature. Managers are usually depicted as people who have the power of formal authority and who are in charge of the organisation or his or her organisational unit (Mintzberg, 1973; Robbins and Mukerji, 1990). Furthermore, they are responsible for the management side of organisations. Management is defined as a process of planning, organising, leading and controlling the work efforts of employees (Robbins and Mukerji, 1990; Stoner et al, 1994). To these functions decision-making, staffing, communicating and motivating may be added (Kreitner, 1995; Massie, 1987). The process of management involves the use of all organisational resources to achieve specific organisational objectives (Evenden and Anderson, 1992; Massie, 1987; Stoner et al, 1994). Thus management is seen as a process, indeed, as a social process (Kreitner, 1995).

It is not useful, however, simply to examine managerial functions in order to understand what shapes a manager. Examining managerial functions in isolation tells us little about what managers actually do. A more fruitful and efficient way of defining managers is to explore the roles they play (Evenden and Anderson, 1992; Kreitner, 1995; Mintzberg, 1973; Robbins and Mukerji, 1990). To do so, it is useful to build on the foundation of the 10 key roles provided by Mintzberg (1973) that managers play. These 10 roles may be classified into three groups, namely, interpersonal, informational and decisional roles (Kreitner, 1995; Robbins and Mukerji, 1990). Interpersonal roles include figurehead, leader and liaison officer. Informational roles include monitor, disseminator and spokesperson. Decisional roles include entrepreneur, disturbance handler, resource allocator and negotiator.

Therefore, a manager may be defined as a person with authority, who is in charge of an organisation or an organisational subsection, and who performs a number of roles and functions that are common to most managerial positions. A manager is part of a social process by which he or she utilises people and material resources to achieve organisational objectives. Managers are shaped by organisational demands to achieve those objectives by the appropriate utilisation of people and other resources. If all this shapes a manager, what shapes a professional?

What Shapes a Professional?

A profession can be distinguished by two criteria (Mintzberg, 1973). The first is a common set of roles and programs for work performance, and the second is knowledge, particularly within a scientific paradigm, which is specific to the organisation and its particular market or industry. There tend to be three general research approaches adopted when studying professions (Landsbury, 1978).

These approaches highlight the trait, institutional and legalistic features of professions (Landsbury, 1978). The trait approach says that professions share common characteristics, such as particular roles and specialised knowledge, and personality traits such as altruism. These characteristics are said to distinguish a profession from other occupations (Landsbury, 1978). It is interesting to note that one disadvantage of adopting this approach is generaliseability. That is, specific professional occupations will not always exhibit all these characteristics.

The institutional approach characterises a profession in terms of a process of institutional or associational development. For an occupation to be defined as a profession, it has to follow a sequence of set events or stages. These stages include: establishing a professional association; changing the name of the occupation; developing an ethical code; obtaining public support through prolonged agitation; and developing training facilities. The Australian Institute of Management (AIM) is an example of an institutional approach to professionalism.

AIM is a non-profit professional management association. Its role is to promote and contribute to the establishment and maintenance of the highest standards of management practice in the community, and to further the recognition of management as an established profession. It has a nationwide membership of more than 23,000 personal members and

5000 corporate members, and offers five nationally accredited certificate programs to members (http://www.aim.com.au).

The legislative approach states that the defining feature of a profession is the recognition of its status by the state. Recognition generally occurs through registration or licensing. For example, psychologists are required to be registered by the appropriate body before they can start or continue to practise. In Australia, the Australian Psychological Society (APS) sees itself as being the premier professional body, with about 13,000 members. Registration, however, is the responsibility of the State and Territory Psychologists Registration Boards, and a person wishing to practice as a psychologist must be legally registered with one of these boards.

Requirements for registering as a psychologist are prescribed by State and Territory Acts that generally require the completion of four full-time years of academic study in psychology and two additional full-time years of post-graduate training or supervised experience (http://www.psychsociety.com.au). This requirement is consistent with the view of Kleinig's (1996) that the institutional approach includes a consistent standard of tertiary education.

By contrast, for Kastens (1980) and Maister (1997) professionals or professionalism is not defined by a set of competencies or the extent of knowledge one has, but by an attitude. Consequently, there is no one theory or definition that provides us with a simple answer about what comprises a profession. While recognising that not all occupations will fit all criteria, the common themes and approaches discussed above will serve as a definition, namely:

- *attitudes:* firstly, professionalism is defined by each individual's attitudes towards his or her role, work colleagues and working environment;
- *competencies and performance:* secondly, professionalism is defined according to the level of competencies and performance attained by an individual, including ongoing professional development, in the completion of a set of common roles and functions;
- *formal recognition by the State*: thirdly, the profession is recognised by the state.

As professionals, it is of interest to note how, in that role, managers treat people with whom they work, and whether or not they are aware of the impact of their actions on other employees. It is also important to ascertain whether or not managers are equipped with a set of competencies and attitudes that enable them to deal effectively with workplace change.

Do Managers 'Shape up' as Professionals?

From the definitions provided, it is evident that managerial jobs do require people to perform a common set of roles, thus meeting the first of Mintzberg's (1973) criteria of what constitutes a profession. The requirement proposed by Kleinig (1996) and Mintzberg (1973), for formal learning in the performance and the implementation of managerial roles, such as that taught in universities and management schools, is less clear. In the Australian context, Karpin (1995) and McCarthy et al (1995) pointed to a paucity of management education, and training and development, especially in terms of the development of people skills. Such skills include teamwork, communication, negotiation and conflict resolution.

Managers are defined by a common set of roles and functions. This is a core characteristic of a profession. According to this characteristic, the occupation of manager is considered to be a profession. In simply meeting this criterion of being in the occupation of manager, however, it cannot be assumed that a manager therefore is a professional. How professional one is, is also dependent on attitude and action. It is difficult to generalise about the personality traits and characteristics of all managers. Therefore, whether or not a manager is professional depends on a set of parameters that guide his or her attitude towards work colleagues, the organisation and the wider social milieu within which work occurs. That milieu includes customers, suppliers, shareholders, lobby and pressure groups, and society at large.

It is of concern that, within these parameters, there is growing evidence to suggest that, in general, managers are *not* professional. In recent years, anecdotal and empirical evidence has emerged relating to abuse of employees by managers. Increasing evidence illustrates the incidence and severity of this issue both at an individual and organisational level. Incidence studies into workplace bullying conducted in England by Rayner (1998, 1999), in the Republic of Ireland by O'Moore et al (1998), and in Wales by Lewis (1999), for example, have revealed that most respondents are bullied or abused by individuals in more powerful positions, such as managers.

A number of studies have identified the negative consequences for employees of workplace abuse. These studies include those from Australia (Barron, 1998; McCarthy et al, 1995; Sheehan, 1996, 1998a, 1999), England (Archer, 1999; Crawford, 1999; Liefooghe and Olafsson, 1999), Finland (Vartia, 1996) and Germany (Zapf, 1999; Zapf et al, 1996). Also included are those from Norway (Einarsen, 1999; Einarsen et al, 1998), the Republic of Ireland (O'Moore et al, 1998; Randall et al, 1999), Sweden (Leymann, 1996), and the USA (Keashly, 1998). Consequences identified include: anxiety, burnout, depression, diminished health and wellbeing, post-traumatic stress disorder, psychological symptoms such as low confidence, low self-esteem, feelings of helplessness and stress.

The costs to organisations of workplace abuse may also be identified. Outcomes of increased absences from work as employees avail themselves of sick leave or other types of leave in their attempt to recover their health, as proposed by McCarthy et al (1995), alert us to organisational costs. Lost working time, expensive legal fees and a need for intervention by external consultants as contributors to organisational costs have been identified as significant costs (Leymann, 1990). Organisational costs may also be inferred from studies by Archer (1999), Crawford (1999), and Liefooghe and Olafsson (1999).

It may therefore be argued that some managers' actions in the workplace are not appropriate within our understanding of managers as professionals. Abuse by managers is an issue that, if left unchecked, can cripple individuals and organisations on several levels, including the financial, physical and psychological. A number of solutions have been suggested for dealing with the problem. Suggestions include ensuring managers abide by their code of conduct (Whitton, 1994); seeking legal redress (Mullany and Handford, 1993); and legislative change (Overall, 1995). It may be inferred from these suggestions that there is a need to address the problem, a need previously asserted by Sheehan (1998b) and Spry (1998).

Reshaping Managers as Professionals

The problem of abuse by managers is a serious issue. If ignored, it may be a costly decision for both the individuals involved and the organisation. Professionals are not only defined by their actions but also by their attitudes and competencies. A manager's attitude towards co-workers and his or her ability to manage often uncertain and ambiguous situations is partly what defines them as a professional. Inadequate people skills may attribute to the problem of workplace abuse by certain managers. A comprehensive approach is required in Australia in order to address the problem. If managers wish to continue to be regarded as professionals, the development of emotional intelligence in managers is now suggested as one solution for addressing the problem.

Strategies for Developing Emotional Intelligence

Emotional intelligence, as suggested by Cooper and Sawaf (1997) and Mayer and Salovey (1993), is a social intelligence that enables people to recognise and differentiate their own and others' emotions and make appropriate choices for thinking and action. As seen in Perkins (1994) and Sternberg (1996), it is an intelligence that managers can learn, develop and improve. In conditions of uncertainty or ambiguity, such as those created by organisational change, our emotions and our inability or unwillingness to recognise and differentiate our own emotional states or the emotional states of others, may become difficult to manage. However, as indicated by Goleman (1996) and Cooper and Sawaf (1997), people often seek what they perceive as an easier path by trying to keep emotions out of tense situations and dealing with matters only on a rational basis.

Emotional intelligence may be seen as occurring at an intra-personal and interpersonal level (Gardner, 1993; Goleman, 1996; and Salovey and Mayer, 1990). At the intra-personal level, using emotional intelligence requires the ability to form an accurate, honest model of oneself and to be able to use that model to operate effectively in life. At the interpersonal level, it requires the ability to understand and work with other people. Development of emotional intelligence in managers dealing with the demands, rapidity and uncertainty of change may help them to become more acutely aware of their own needs and the needs of others. This will assist managers with the crucial task of managing process (Bodi et al, 1997; Salovey and Mayer, 1990).

Emotional intelligence is instrumental in process situations because it allows for the expression and legitimisation of sensations, emotions and even 'gut feelings' people so often experience when in social interaction or during private reflections. The process of legitimising feelings does not involve the expression of them in an anti-social, manipulative or violent way, but in ways that open dialogue and promote the non-defensive yet challenging discussion of people's actions, words and assumptions (Weisinger, 1998). Effective communication tools are critical for enabling managers to successfully manage process and for developing their emotional intelligence. These tools include active listening, expressive actions and interaction management (Dick, 1991; Kaye, 1994).

To be readily available to managers, the development of emotional intelligence needs to begin before entering the workforce. Introducing this concept and encouraging the development of emotional intelligence in universities and management schools, and in programs conducted by professional bodies, would better equip those people entering management positions with more effective communication and emotional intelligence abilities. Furthermore, for those already in management positions, the development of emotional intelligence may help them learn to deal with their emotions and others' emotions in more appropriate, empathic ways, rather than resorting to abuse. Introducing strategies to develop emotional intelligence would contribute to managers once again being seen as professionals. Moreover, if managers act more appropriately and professionally towards employees, those actions increase the likelihood of developing more productive, efficient and healthy organisations. We are well aware that those are the goals to which most organisations aspire.

References

Archer, D (1999) 'Exploring "Bullying" Culture in the Para-Military Organisation' 20(1/2) *International Journal of Manpower* 94–105.

Barron, O (1998) 'The Distinction between Workplace Bullying and Workplace Violence and the Ramifications for OHS' 14(6) *Journal of Occupational Health and Safety* 575–80.

Bodi, A, Maggs, G and Edgar, D (1997) *When Too Much Change is Never Enough*. Sydney: Business and Professional Publishing.

Cooper, R (1997) 'Applying Emotional Intelligence in the Workplace' 51(12) *Training and Development* 31–8.

Cooper, R and Sawaf, A (1997) *Executive EQ: Emotional Intelligence in Leadership and Organizations*. New York: Grosset/Putnam.

Crawford, N (1999) 'Conundrums and Confusion in Organisations: The Etymology of the Work "Bully"' 20(1/2) *International Journal of Manpower* 86–93.

Dick, B (1991) *Helping Groups to be Effective*. Brisbane: Interchange.

Einarsen, S (1999) 'The Nature and Causes of Bullying at Work' 20(1/2) *International Journal of Manpower* 16–27.

Einarsen, S, Matthiesen, S and Skogstad, A (1998) 'Bullying, Burnout and Well-Being among Assistant Nurses' 14(6) *Journal of Occupational Health and Safety: Australia and New Zealand* 563–8.

Evenden, R and Anderson, G (1992) *Management Skills*. Workingham: Addison-Wesley.

Gardner, H (1993) *Multiple Intelligences: The Theory in Practice*. New York: Basic Books.

Goleman, D (1996) *Emotional Intelligence*. London: Bloomsbury.

Karpin, D (1995) *Enterprising Nation: Executive Summary*. Canberra: AGPS.

Kastens, ML (1980) *Redefining the Manager's Job: The Proactive Manager in a Reactive World*. New York: AMACOM.

Kaye, M (1994) *Communication Management*. Sydney: Prentice Hall.

Keashly, L (1998) 'Emotional Abuse in the Workplace' 1(1) *Journal of Emotional Abuse* 85–117.

Kleinig, J (1996) *The Ethics of Policing*. Cambridge: Cambridge University Press.

Kreitner, D (1995) *Management* (6th edn). Toronto: Houghton Mifflin.

Landsbury, R (1978) *Professionals and Management: A Study of Behaviour in Organizations*. Brisbane: University of Queensland Press.

Lewis, D (1999) 'Workplace Bullying: Interim Findings of a Study in Further and Higher Education in Wales' 20(1/2) *International Journal of Manpower* 106–18.

Leymann, H (1990) 'Mobbing and Psychological Terror at Workplaces' 5(2) *Violence and Victims* 119–26.

Leymann, H (1996) 'The Content and Development of Mobbing at Work' 5(2) *European Journal of Work and Organizational Psychology* 165–84.
Liefooghe, A and Olafsson, R (1999) '"Scientists" and "Amateurs": Mapping the Bullying Domain' 20(1/2) *International Journal of Manpower* 39–49.
McCarthy, P, Sheehan, M and Kearns, D (1995) *Managerial Styles and Their Effects on Employees' Health and Well-Being in Organisations Undergoing Restructuring*. Brisbane: School of Organisational Behaviour and Human Resource Management, Griffith University.
Maister, DH (1997) *True Professionalism: The Courage to Care about Your People, Your Clients, and Your Career*. New York: Free Press.
Massie, J (1987) *Essentials of Management* (4th edn). Englewood Cliffs, NJ: Prentice Hall International.
Mayer, JD and Salovey, P (1993) *The Intelligence of Emotional Intelligence* 17(4) *Intelligence* 433–42.
Mintzberg, H (1973) *The Nature of Managerial Work*. New York: Harper & Row.
Mintzberg, H (1989) *Mintzberg on Management: Inside Our Strange World of Organizations*. New York: Free Press.
Mullany, NJ and Handford, PR (1993) *Tort Liability for Psychiatric Damage*. Sydney: Law Book Company.
O'Moore, M, Seigne, E, McGuire, L and Smith, M (1998) 'Victims of Bullying at Work in Ireland' 14(6) *Journal of Occupational Health and Safety: Australia and New Zealand* 569–74.
Overall, S (1995) 'Union Demands Action to Stop Bullying at Work', *Personnel Management,* 21 September, p 10.
Perkins, D (1994) *Outsmarting IQ: The Emerging Science of Learnable Intelligence*. New York: Free Press.
Peters, T (1993) *Liberation Management*. London: Pan Books.
Peters, J and Smith, P (1998) 'Learn to Ask the Right Questions' 10(3) *Journal of Workplace Learning* 169–72.
Randall, P, Seigne, E and Coyne, I (1999) 'Personality Traits of the Victims of Workplace Bullying'. Conference paper presented at European Congress on Work and Organisational Psychology Conference, Helsinki, 12–15 May.
Rayner, C (1998) 'Workplace Bullying: Do Something!' 14(6) *Journal of Occupational Health and Safety: Australia and New Zealand* 581–5.
Rayner, C (1999) 'From Research to Implementation: Finding Leverage for Prevention' 20(1/2) *International Journal of Manpower* 28–38.
Robbins, S and Mukerji, D (1990) *Managing Organisations*. New York: Prentice Hall.
Salovey, P and Mayer, J (1990) 'Emotional Intelligence' 9(3) *Imagination, Cognition, and Personality* 185–211.
Sheehan, M (1996) 'Case Studies in Organisational Restructuring', in P McCarthy, M Sheehan and W Wilkie (eds), *Bullying: From Backyard to Boardroom*. Sydney: Millennium.
Sheehan, M (1998a) 'Restructuring Rhetoric versus Reality', in P McCarthy, M Sheehan, S Wilkie and W Wilkie (eds), *Bullying: Causes, Costs, and Cures*. Brisbane: BBA.
Sheehan, M (1998b) 'Bullying: Signs and Solutions', in C Rayner, M Sheehan and M Barker (eds), *Bullying at Work: 1998 Research Update*. Stafford: Staffordshire University Business School.

Sheehan, M (1999) 'Workplace Bullying: Responding with Some Emotional Intelligence' 20(1/2) *International Journal of Manpower* 57–69.

Spry, M (1998) 'Workplace Harassment: What is it, and What Should the Law do about it?' 40(2) *Journal of Industrial Relations* 232–46.

Sternberg, R (1996) *Successful Intelligence*. New York: Simon & Schuster.

Stoner, J, Yetton, P, Craig, J and Johnston, KD (1994) *Management* (2nd edn). Sydney: Prentice Hall.

Vartia, M (1996) 'The Sources of Bullying: Psychological Work Environment and Organizational Climate' 5(2) *European Journal of Work and Organizational Psychology* 203–14.

Weisinger, H (1998) *Emotional Intelligence at Work*. San Francisco: Jossey Bass.

Whitton, H (1994) 'The Rediscovery of Professional Ethics for Public Officials: An Australian Overview', in N Preston (ed), *Ethics for the Public Sector*. Sydney: Federation Press.

Zapf, D (1999) 'Organisational, Work Group Related and Personal Causes of Mobbing/Bullying at Work' 20(1/2) *International Journal of Manpower* 70–85.

Zapf, D, Knorz, C and Kulla, M (1996) 'On the Relationship between Mobbing Factors and Job Content: The Social Work Environment and Health Outcomes' 5(2) *European Journal of Work and Organizational Psychology* 215–37.

Chapter 13

Bullying the Elderly

Trish Bulbeck

Introduction

Elder abuse is one of today's best hidden problems. Australian statistics indicate that as many as 5% of the population over the age of 65 could be subject to some form of mistreatment by someone they trust.[1] Older people are bullied, intimidated, ignored, neglected and abused physically, emotionally, sexually and financially. They are neglected by family members and overlooked in the workforce. Although government departments in Australia know that elder abuse exists and some token programs are funded to address this problem, Australia is about 15 years behind other Western nations in its funding of services. New Zealand has been developing strategies and services to confront the problem for more than a decade, so why is Australia so far behind? Do we care what is happening to elderly people in this country?

This chapter will address three issues that are important in raising awareness of elder abuse. Firstly, it will give a broad summary of elder abuse and what is happening in Australia in comparison with other Western nations. Secondly, it will take a brief look at suggestions for appropriate legislation for preventing elder abuse; and thirdly, it will give some examples of what is happening throughout Australia to our aged population, that is, those people over the age of 65.

Elder Abuse

Elder abuse is the international term given to abuse of an older person by someone they trust. It is rarely reported for a number of reasons: the older person may feel ashamed that a close family member is mistreating them; the older person may fear retaliation from the person or persons mistreating them; the person may believe he or she is the only one suffering at the hands of a family member, or someone else they trust. Our social and emotional attitude to ageing and negative stereotyping of older people has contributed to keeping the problem of elder abuse hidden in our communities.[2]

A number of factors contribute to abuse occurring. They include: the physical and emotional dependence on others by the older person; ongoing relationship problems between the older person and their adult children; gambling problems, alcohol dependency or drugs; a mental disease in either the abused or the abuser; the suspected abuser's financial dependence on the older person; or a severely stressed carer.[3] These conditions are accepted worldwide as the main contributing factors.

What have also evolved are workplace experiences of abuse for older people who remain in the workforce, which once respected those older and more experienced workers. Some employers and fellow employees are becoming bullies of older workers to such an extent that older people in the workforce can no longer expect to be free from intimidation.[4] New technology and business techniques have left older people without training as young people enter the workforce with high levels of technological skills.

The ageist assumption that older people are unable to understand new technology or business processes can have a physical and emotional impact on older people. This can be detrimental to both the mental and physical health of older workers. There may also be a negative financial impact on older people who feel compelled to leave their workplace. Older people can be forced into retirement with little opportunity to contribute sufficiently to their superannuation, and ultimately they become dependent on the old-age pension, which can lead to the negative perception of the elderly as 'burdens on society', especially by the media.

Elder abuse can also occur where there has been continuing domestic violence. It may occur where there is a shift in the power within the relationship, and I believe there is a distinction between elder abuse and domestic violence. For example, a wife may have been able to run from her bullying husband in the past, but an age-related illness now reduces her mobility, so she is caught and physically or emotionally mistreated. Or the abusing husband may develop dementia and the wife discovers she is now in a position to take revenge, and inflicts physical abuse on him or neglects him. Both situations indicate a move from domestic violence to elder abuse.

Emotional abuse is involved in most situations where elder abuse occurs, most often through verbal intimidation, humiliation, harassment or ignoring an older person. It can induce feelings of shame, indignity and powerlessness.[5] One reported incident from the workplace occurred when the senior female person required something from a subordinate's office, which was on another floor of a building with no lift. The subordinate, an older person, was informed that the senior person would go to save time, which left the subordinate feeling ashamed of his inability to keep pace physically with younger staff. Emotional abuse can also be inflicted through non-verbal intimidation.

The financial aspect of elder abuse occurs when the assets of an older person are improperly used. Sometimes the older person will be unaware of it if they have given an Enduring Power of Attorney to someone they trust. That form of financial abuse can occasionally occur when a trusted member of the family is the attorney and uses the older person's money or property for their own purposes.

Sexual abuse is often left unreported, although it has been reported to various agencies in Queensland in a number of instances. It is emotionally distressing when it occurs and can be physically damaging; in some of these situations the abused person has been taken out of her own home and placed in a nursing home, which is not a desirable outcome, especially as sexual abuse is also reported to occur in aged care facilities.

Physical abuse occurs through slapping, pushing, pulling or any other act that causes harm. Examples of malicious acts of bullying include pushing an older person along whilst they carry a lighted cigarette and withholding heaters during winter months. Being careless in assisting a nursing home resident in and out of bed can cause fragile skin to tear. Some medical interventions, such as taking an old person's blood pressure, can leave painful bruising, and this is a form of systemic abuse, because it is the accepted method of measuring the person's blood pressure.

The frailty of very old age can leave these people vulnerable to all forms of abuse. Although our population has been ageing for some time now, there is still little public or professional awareness of the changed physical and emotional needs of older people. This lack of knowledge can lead to serious neglect and mishandling of older individuals.

Since a number of reports on elder abuse have been published, some attention has been paid to the problem. Some reports are specific and refer only to people in institutional care, but others, such as the report issued in Queensland in 1994 by the Office of Ageing, examined the abuse that older people were experiencing in their own homes.[6]

Early in 1990, before publication of the Queensland report, a number of concerned aged care workers in south-east Queensland banded together under the auspices of the Queensland Council of Carers. They shared their concerns about what they were seeing in the community and sought interstate and overseas material to gain an insight into this 'new' social problem. They united with a handful of government department representatives to form a taskforce to examine the intimidation and abuse of older people.

Concurrently, the results of the first recognised elder abuse research were published in New South Wales. This research was carried out by an aged care assessment service, with geriatrician Susan Kurrle and social worker Paul Sadler. Their results were similar to those from other Western nations, where slightly less than 5% of the aged populations were found to be subject to elder abuse.[7] Other research in Australia has examined more specific issues such as relationships in caring, past marital relationships and the difference between elder abuse and domestic violence.[8]

Programs that are currently available in Australia offer education and training, and most of them focus on the development of protocols for individual agencies. The programs are somewhat sporadic – the NSW program ended in mid-1998, leaving a training kit and video for use by agencies. The Western Australian program was completed in 1999, and a private consultant offers a program throughout Victoria, as well as several agency services. Queensland and South Australia have government-funded programs, and Queensland offers a helpline for older people. Both programs offer assessment and referral, as well as support and education for case workers. Each State funds the equivalent of three full-time positions.

When this level of funding is compared with funding provided for domestic violence and child abuse programs, it becomes apparent that governments and bureaucrats are demonstrating a disregard for the needs of those older people suffering elder abuse. Students have not been attracted to gerontological studies in medicine, nursing, social sciences, welfare or allied health in the numbers needed, and this could be due to the ageist attitude that permeates our society and which should be of major concern.

By comparison to Australia, New Zealand, with a population of 3.8 million, had 22 elder abuse programs operating by February 2001. The programs are located throughout both north and south islands, and offer a range of services from case work to support groups.[9] They are attached to 22 geriatric and rehabilitation services, although only one is funded by the New Zealand Health Department. The New Zealand Department of Social Welfare funds the other services.

Canada and the USA have also been actively seeking solutions to the problem of elder abuse for more than 20 years. In some provinces of

Canada and most States of the USA, reporting of elder abuse is mandatory.[10] The programs offered by the USA include a well-staffed financial service in California, and a well-funded perpetrator program to counsel perpetrators of elder abuse and prevent further mistreatment of the elderly. Interestingly, the manager of the perpetrator program in Los Angeles reported that she had found a program developed in Western Australia to be one of the best she had studied.[11] She was able to apply certain aspects of the Australian program to the Los Angeles one to achieve successful outcomes.

The Australian program was piloted by Gosnells Council in Perth, but it has not attracted further funding in Western Australia or anywhere else in Australia, despite having great potential as a preventive measure for governments and for providing an improved quality of life for older people currently being abused.

Canada has a range of programs, beginning in the schools. The junior school programs are based on teaching respect for all people, especially older people. The high school programs focus on developing respect for oneself and all others. These programs operating successfully in Canada are based on research.[12] Teams of workers in the programs usually contain someone with a legal background or a police officer, a social worker or psychologist, and sometimes a nurse. There is always a mixture of skills and knowledge. Older people are sometimes team members, generally as volunteers, and the Seniors (Victims) Support Network is one of the many programs operating in Canada where older people support each other through education and information sharing.

One example of volunteers working within a police station had excellent results in Canada. A number of older people were falling victim to the crime of telefraud, which is where perpetrators of telefraud belong to a highly organised group which obtains money from individuals under false pretences. They prey on vulnerable older people by developing an empathetic relationship with the older person, which leads that older person to trusting them. Because trust is involved, it becomes elder abuse, as well as being a criminal act. Police called for a number of volunteers from the seniors' organisations to be trained to help them attack this problem. The volunteers would go to the police station where they would ring the known victims and talk to them about it. Each volunteer was given two or three names and telephone numbers to ring, under the supervision of a police sergeant. Sometimes the victim preferred to continue to receive the telephone calls from the telefraud operator despite police intervention, and continued to send cheques to them, as they were the most constant contact they had with the outside world.

In England one of the most successful programs is the Accessline for older people who believe they are experiencing elder abuse (the Queensland Helpline closely follows the training and operation of this system). England and Ireland have considerable research and training material available to assist the development of policies and practices to confront elder abuse. Norway and Japan also both conduct research and offer programs. South Africa and a number of countries in South America, such as Brazil and Argentina, have active workers for elder abuse prevention, although they are hampered by their social and political systems, which reportedly contain graft and corruption at the highest levels of government, in the armed forces and in the police. It has led to the poverty and neglect of millions of indigenous people, frequently of those who survive into old age, and is part of systemic neglect that has only recently begun to be addressed.

Legislation to Prevent Elder Abuse

Legislation that specifically protects older people from abuse is generally available in most States and Territories through domestic violence or family violence legislation. The Queensland *Domestic Violence (Family Protection) Act* 1989 has been reviewed during the 1990s to provide more protection for older people. An infrastructure to support older people under the Act now needs to be developed. Overseas examples of refuges for men and women, especially one developed within the Kerby Centre in Calgary, Canada, could provide a great example to Australians.

Australian States and Territories also have guardianship legislation, the newest being in Queensland in 2000, where a Guardianship Tribunal has been appointed. That is designed to protect the rights of people who are unable to make their own decisions. It is especially useful legislation for the protection of older people who may lose their cognitive capacity through a dementia or some other age-related disease. Currently in Queensland the Adult Guardian has comprehensive investigative power to examine suspected abuse of a person who has lost their ability to make their own decisions in lifestyle, health and financial matters.

The Nature of Elder Abuse

Some examples of elder abuse range from the criminal act of murder, through medical mistreatment by doctors, nurses and allied health professionals, to the attitude of families towards their seniors' possessions.

Case 1: The horrific murder of an elderly woman on the Gold Coast by her grandson, early in 1997, was well documented in the media. The grandson was on drugs and regularly forced his grandmother to give him her pension so he could buy drugs. He later killed her and placed her body in a laundry basket. Before he became addicted to drugs the grandson reportedly had a loving relationship with his grandmother.

Case 2: An elderly woman was admitted to a public hospital to await rehabilitation in a geriatric unit. She had broken a bone in her foot. Three days after her admission she was visited by a daughter who had travelled from interstate. She found her mother dehydrated and very confused. Her face appeared disjointed – her upper denture was causing pain and she was not eating.

Some time later, after her daughter had returned interstate, a patient who had been in a bed opposite took note of the woman's unusual surname and checked the telephone directory. She telephoned an individual whose surname was the same and who turned out to be the woman's son. She told him she believed the hospital staff were leaving the elderly woman to die. More than six weeks later doctors diagnosed a dislocated jaw.

Case 3. An active 76-year-old woman offered her only son the use of a large granny flat under her home. While she was away visiting relatives, the son moved his family's belongings upstairs and his mother's down to the granny flat. She was devastated on her return but was fearful of losing her son's love if she complained. He informed his mother that since she lived alone it was better if he and his young family of three moved into the more spacious area, as it was going to be his eventually in any case.

Conclusion

Elder abuse is a social issue that is hidden. Society needs to acknowledge its existence, and older people need to know how to avoid it. Longstanding attitudes in society have led to our becoming an ageist society, causing considerable physical and emotional problems for older people. The majority of perpetrators of elder abuse use every form of bullying possible. Other perpetrators do so through neglect or negligence. Older workers can be at risk of losing employment and are vulnerable to intimidation in the workplace.

Australia has much to achieve before our policies and programs catch up with those of other Western societies in addressing elder abuse. A major concern, ageism, must to be fought quickly and strongly to prevent its further damaging the lives of older people.

Notes

1 Dr Darcy Kelly encouraged health professionals to study the emerging trends in elder abuse while he was the Director of the Bureau for Extended Care in the State Health Department during the 1980s in Kelly, 1992.

2 Professor Sean McCarthy and Trish Bulbeck have challenged mental health workers to examine their attitudes and treatment of elderly people in Bulbeck and McCarthy, 1993.

3 Paul Sadler, a social worker involved in research with Dr Susan Kurrle and Dr Ian Cameron, was instrumental in developing a model of intervention for use in identified elder abuse cases in Kurrle et al, 1991.

4 Betty Friedan examines ageing from her own perspective and provides a wealth of information on the ageing process in Friedan, 1993.

5 See Jan Meares (1997) for an examination of the issue of elder abuse within a feminist framework.

6 This report followed community consultations throughout the State (Office of Ageing, 1994).

7 The *Australian Medical Journal* recognised the research of Kurrle et al (1991).

8 See Hughes (1996), for an examination of the conflict and violence that can occur in caring relationships.

9 Jenni Nana (1999) presented the New Zealand report to the Oceania Representative for the International Network for the Prevention of Elder Abuse.

10 Dr Rosalie Wolfe is recognised as a world leader in elder abuse research and is a consultant for many US and international bodies examining family violence, legislation and prevention programs (see Wolfe, 1997).

11 Beth Kingsley and Susan Johnson united their nursing and social work skills in researching issues affecting older people (see Kingsley and Johnson, 1995).

12 The discussion paper prepared by L McDonald and A Collins is an example of the level of research frequently found in Canada (Mcdonald and Collins 1998).

Bibliography

Bulbeck, T (1998) 'Ageing with Respect and Dignity: When Dreams are not Reality' 2 *Domestic Violence, Action and Resources: The Magazine* (June), pp 13–14.

Bulbeck, T and McCarthy, S (1993) 'The Hidden Epidemic'. Paper presented at North Queensland Mental Health Conference, Communicate to Break through the Barriers, Hamilton Island, 18–20 March.

Field, AM (1996) *Financial Exploitation of Older People in Their Homes* (Discussion Paper 2). Sydney: NSW Advisory Committee on Abuse of Older People.

Fielding, W (1999) 'Elder Abuse: How Do We Prevent the Phenomenon of the Nineties becoming the Uncontrolled Crime of the 21st Century?' Paper presented at the International Homecare and HACC Australia Conference, Brisbane, 29 March–1 April.

Friedan, B (1993) *The Fountain of Age*. London: Random House, p 168.

Hughes, M (1996) 'Conflict in Caring: An Investigation of Conflict, Violence and Abuse in Older People's Caregiving Relationships'. PhD thesis, School of Social Work and Social Policy, University of Queensland.

Kelly, D (1992) 'Identifying Physical Abuse, Sexual Abuse and Neglect in Older People: Implications for Medical and Health Care Professionals', in *Dignity and Security: Proceedings from Conference*. Brisbane: Queensland Taskforce on Elder Abuse Prevention, pp 49–54.

Kingsley, B and Johnson, S (1995) 'Resolving Elder Abuse: Issues Arising from a Perpetrator Program' 13(4) *Australian Journal on Ageing* 172–8.

Kurrle, S (1993) 'Elder Abuse: A Hidden Problem' *Modern Medicine of Australia* (September) 58–62.

Kurrle, S, Sadler, P and Cameron, I (1991) 'Elder Abuse: An Australian Case Series' 155 *Medical Journal of Australia* (August) 149–57.

McDonald, L and Collins, A (1998) *Elder Abuse and Neglect: A Discussion Paper for Health Canada*. Toronto: Centre for Applied Social Research, University of Toronto, p 2.

Meares, J (1997) *Triple Jeopardy: Gender and Abuse of Older People* (Discussion Paper 5). Sydney: NSW Advisory Committee on Abuse of Older People, p 6.

Nana, J (1999) *Evaluation of Elder Abuse Services in New Zealand*. Wellington: Department of Social Welfare.

Office of Ageing (1994) *Abuse of Older People in Queensland: A Report of the Project on Abuse of Older People*. Brisbane: Department of Family Services, Aboriginal and Islander Affairs.

Sadler, P (1993) 'Patterns of Elder Abuse'. Paper presented at Australian Institute of Criminology Conference, Crime and Older People, Adelaide, 24 February.

Wolfe, R (1997) 'National Committee for the Prevention of Elder Abuse'. Presented at the Round Table creating an International Network at the Sixteenth International Conference of Gerontology, Adelaide, 20 August.

Index